DON'T FORGET

What Drug & Insurance Companies Don't Want You To Know About Memory Loss!

L   w   o   R
O
  s   D
S
                              C o
                                  n

for....get....ful.......ness   fu
                                        s i o n

Jill Joyce, Ph.D.

The Shocking Truths About Anti-Aging, Prevention, and Recovery of Mild to Severe Memory Loss Due to Normal Aging, Stroke, Head-Injury, Alzheimer's, etc.

with

True Family Stories

www.dontforgetmemoryloss.com

SWP

Copyright ©2003

SWP Still Waters Publications

8983 SE Sunfish Place
Hobe Sound, FL 33455

P.O. Box 670686
Coral Springs, FL 33067

Website: www.dontforgetmemoryloss.com
E-mail: dontforget@bellsouth.net

All rights reserved. No part of this book may be reproduced, translated, stored in a retrieval system, or transmitted in any form or by any means, electronic or mechanical, including photocopying, microfilming, recording, or otherwise, without written permission from the author or publisher, except for the inclusion of brief quotations in review.

Copyright ©2003 by Jill Joyce
First edition 2003
Printed in the United States of America
　　　Library of Congress Cataloging-in-Publication 2003097863
Joyce, Jill

Don't Forget: What Drug and Insurance Companies Don't Want You To Know About Memory Loss. Subtitle: The Shocking Truth About Prevention and Recovery of Mild to Severe Memory Loss due to Aging, Stroke, Head-Injury, Alzheimer's, etc., by Jill Joyce – 1st ed.
ISBN 0-9746252-7-2 (Soft cover)
Includes five appendices, bibliography, index, and researched quotes.

(Research version) Aphasia: Using Narrative to Deal with Lost Narrative Abilities by Jill Joyce (AKA: Jill Joyce-Becker) Includes references and appendices. **TX 5-225-319** ©1999
This publication is sold with the understanding that the publisher and author are not engaged in rendering professional or medical advice or services via this book. A physician should be consulted before adopting any suggestions herein for illnesses. The author and publisher disclaim liability arising directly or indirectly from use of this book.

Dedication

To my family; Alexis & Jonathan Becker, my children; & to Lili's family—You are all my deepest source of warmth, courage & inspiration.

And in memory of my dearest & most missed friend, Lili Giangrandi, who continues to inspire & encourage all who knew her from the heavens & who lives on in our hearts every moment. May her tribute teach us all the art of healing & living:

A truer friend & example I've never known. She loved family, laughter, dancing, art, kindness, hospitality, flowers, wide-brimmed hats, helping people, learning, being in the water on Miami Beach, hearty greetings, encouraging others, giving to the needy, & thanking God—wow! A grateful & forgiving life is a healing life. Quick to forget what is petty, likely to remember what is fun...............

But never—to be forgotten.

May 27, 1957- January 6, 2003

Acknowledgements

To some of the most wonderful people I have ever known. First and foremost, a very special thank you goes to Dr. Margo Weiss. I am forever grateful for her inspiration, wisdom, intelligence, creativity, wit and the numerous hours she poured over this work. Also, thank you to the wonderful families and students I worked with and met over the years, who contributed so much to the making of this book. Thank you to my dear friend, Dr. Helene van Heden, who also read for me and encouraged me always. To Joseph Garrity Esquire, I owe thanks for handling my legal affairs with grace and amazing ease. To Lidia Roig, mother of Lili, for her abiding friendship, hospitality, many kindnesses and for reading with such interest while prodding me to publish. To Roy Lightner for his readings, promotion, and enlightenment. To Dr. Ron Chenail and Dr. Chris Burnett for their readings and pertinent insights. To Foojan Zeine, Kathleen Derrig-Palumbo, Pat Love, and James Alexander, I am so very grateful for your direction, interest, and ideas. To Bob Burg for reading and giving many pointers. To Tina and Dan Lukey for help with the publication and exhortation. To the Serendipity Shop authors and poets for great ideas. To Richard Springler and Bill Wilson for proof reading and ideas. To John Bryans for development. To Eric Stahl for photography. To my sister-in-law, Jeanine Joyce, who has lived through memory loss illness with her parents, for all the brain-storming and support. To Joni Eareckson Tada for her encouragement. To Anthony Robbins for that amazing wheat grass! And to my mother, I thank God for your amazing spirit, abiding love, health, and memory.

About the Author

With experience and research spanning nearly 30 years in dealing with memory loss, Dr. Jill Joyce continues to make memory loss prevention and recovery the focus of her post-doctoral research, ongoing therapy, and university courses on anti-aging, memory loss, and sensation and perception. Her clinical experiences with hospitalized, nursing home, and home bound memory loss patients taught her—memory loss cases are unique, fascinating, and correctable. She is excited that research now corroborates what therapists have already known. The brain heals!

Now she compiles her thoughts and research in this book, <u>Don't Forget: What Drug and Insurance Companies Don't Want You To Know About Memory Loss</u>, written to educate all of us about the hidden agendas and lost truths behind the memory loss epidemic in a straightforward manner. She believes the greatest challenge to conquering elderly and other memory loss problems is mainly a lack of understanding and awareness. <u>Don't Forget</u> is intended to help the public realize that many senseless, unwarranted memory loss situations are plaguing individuals and their families. <u>Don't Forget</u>'s simple explanations, facts, and stories can help, especially through memory loss illnesses.

Dr. Joyce is dual licensed in Psychotherapy and Speech/Language Pathology. She received her PhD at Nova Southeastern University in Marriage and Family Therapy and her Masters degree from the University of Miami. In 1973, she began working with memory loss related to stroke, learning disabilities, and head injury and continued for the first 20 years of her career. Since her doctoral training, she has expanded her practice to include work with anxiety, depression, relationships, weight loss, marriage, pre-marriage, and divorce. She also coaches in life and learning management.

Table of Contents

Dedication.. iii
Acknowledgements.. iv
About the Author... v
Table of Contents.. vi
Introduction... xvii
Those Who Care—Can................................. xxi

Part One... 1
**Chapter I: Causes of Memory Loss—
What's in a Name**..2
Memory Loss Diagnosis...................................3
Memory Loss Therapy After Stroke or Head Injury. 3
Memory Loss Therapy After Alzheimer's............. 4
Alzheimer's or Age-Associated Memory Loss?...... 5
Inappropriateness of Dementia Label 5
Need to Know Diagnostic Classifications............. 6
Start the Mental Exercises................................ 6
Informing or Not Informing Families of the Nature
of Memory Loss?.. 7
Consequences of Not Informing........................ 7
The State of Our Nation's Hospitals and Memory
Loss Protocol.. 8
Hard Realities and Reasons for Hope................... 9
Family Involvement.. 9
Critical Need for Education, Awareness, Solutions...10

**Chapter II: Anti-Aging and Overlooked
Memory Losses**..12
Save Your Brain with an Ounce of Prevention—
the Anti-Aging Regimen 12

A Digestible Basic for Memory Health................ 12
PS/Vital to the Prescription.................................13
Valuable Memory Enhancements...................... 13
Juicing... 14
Mercury and Aluminum Toxins........................ 14
Anesthesia, Drugs, and Alcohol........................ 15
Cigarettes.. 16
Coffee..16
Benzodiazepines, Prozac, and Legal Drugs............ 17
Marijuana...18
Anger, Anxiety, Stress, and Depression................18
Reasons for Wheat Grass...................................... 19
Drug Companies.. 19
My Mom's Age Associated Memory Impairment... 21
Wheat Grass, PS, and Tony Robbins...................22
Recipes..23
Vitamins and Coumadin—What We Did 24
Waiting for the Cure... 25
Is Alzheimer's Genetic?......................................26
Other Often Overlooked Forms of Memory Loss......26
ADHD...27
Brain Tumors/ HIV... 27
The Drug Company Protocol............................28
Thyroid Disorders.. 29
Epilepsy.. 31
Hormone Imbalance...32

**Chapter III: The Keep It Simple—
Facts of Serious Memory Loss**......................... 33
Three-Hour Time Line Needed to Prevent Further
Brain Damage with Stroke..............................33

Stroke and Brain Injury Symptoms...................... 33
Alzheimer's, Acetylcholine, and the Hippocampus.. 34
What Will Insurance Companies Do Next? 35
Realistic Time Lines for Recovery...................... 36
Can You Get Them Back After Memory Loss........ 37
Family Solutions... 38
Some Memory Loss Compensation Methods 38
True Family Stories and Dialogues 39
The Foreign Language Metaphor and
Unlocking a Door for Memory Loss 40

Chapter IV: Like the Traveling
Language Student........... 41
Being Understood.. 41
The Hospital Stay Discoveries........................... 41
Locked Inside Without a Voice......................... 42
The Confusing Journey Begins!.........................44
Confusing Journeys that Happen with
Normal Memory 44
Use It or Lose It... 44
Some Helpful Activities and Computer Devices
for Language and Memory Reconditioning............ 45
Professional Speech Therapy & Memory
Loss Planning... 47
Medicare... 47
Variety is the Spice of Life.............................. 47
Assisting without Working Side-by-Side.............. 48
Slow Down, Pause, and Wait for Eye Contact........ 49
Plateaus Happen—Be Patient—Forward
Acceleration Will Return................................ 50
No Pressure in Public, Please, & Think
Before Talking for Them................................. 51

Prompting the First Sound............................... 51
Comparing Normal Language Memory and
Development.. 52
A Refresher Course.. 52
Talking and Working Together at Home............... 53
Computers... 53
Nix Negativity.. 54
Vital! Memory Loss Support Groups
and E-Mail... 54
The Hard Lessons—Normal Memory or
Relearned—Require Patience & Humor............... 55
Expectant Attitude Point I: The Veil of Disability or
Challenge and Love of Learning....................... 57
Expectant Attitude Point II: To Journey is Better
than to Arrive... 58
How to Come Home....................................... 60
Demographics.. 60
A Family Problem: Listen in as One Spouse
Expresses Her Serious Frustration...................... 61
Can You Relate?... 61
Imagine You on that Bed................................. 62
A Student's Surgery—
A Moment of Gratitude.................................. 62
Memory Loss Assumptions with Ventilator
Problems—Damaging Untrue Remarks............... 63
Don't Let Last Words be Lost Words.................. 64
Comprehension is Often in Tact........................ 64

Part Two.. 66
**Chapter V: True Family Stories with
Insurance Affects**.. 67
Overlapping Losses.. 67

Who Spoke During Interviews...........…............68
Clay's Recovery..68
Neurological Repair.......................................69
Stem Cell Research.......................…..............70
Insurance Problems without Recovery Guarantees... 70
Doctor and Therapist Reports...........................70
Family Conversations.....................................71
Meet the Families Who Spoke.........................72
Education Levels...73
Dying...74
Spiritual Coping..75
Agreement without Hesitation about Memory Loss.. 75
Individual Family Profiles...............................75
Family One: Bob (the radio announcer) and Kay.... 75
Family Two: Clay (the CEO) and Pam.............….. 77
Family Three: Sarah & Eve (mother/daughter team) 78
Family Four: Steve (pilot/executive) & Laura........ 79
Eleven Concerns: Families with Memory Loss 80

Chapter VI: 1-11 Eleven Concerns of Families with Language Memory Loss............................... 82

Subchapter VI-1: Family expectations, understanding of language memory loss, lack of education and information... 82
Family One: Bob (the radio announcer) and Kay..... 84
Family Two: Clay (the CEO) and Pam................... 85
Family Three: Sarah & Eve (mother/daughter team) 88
Family Four: Steve (pilot/executive) & Laura......... 94
Reflections on family expectations, understanding of memory loss, & lack of education & information. 98

Subchapter VI-2: Perspective of families—Value given to communication & need for vocal memory loss rehabilitation 100
Family One: Bob (the radio announcer) and Kay….. 100
Family Two: Clay (the CEO) and Pam…................ 102
Family Three: Sarah & Eve (mother/daughter team) 105
Family Four: Steve (pilot/executive) & Laura…….. 106
Reflections on value given to communication and need for vocal rehabilitation 107

Subchapter VI-3: Specific language, memory, comprehension, speech, vocal losses & improvements... 109
Family One: Bob (the radio announcer) and Kay…. 109
Family Two: Clay (the CEO) and Pam…............... 111
Family Three: Sarah & Eve (mother/daughter team)113
Family Four: Steve (pilot/executive) and Laura….... 115
Reflections on specific language, speech, vocal losses and improvements…............................... 117

Subchapter VI-4. Speech/language therapy and language memory loss improvement methods....... 118
Family One: Bob (the radio announcer) and Kay…. 118
Family Two: Clay (the CEO) and Peg…................ 120
Family Three: Sarah & Eve (mother/daughter team) 122
Family Four: Steve (pilot executive) & Laura…….. 125
Reflections: Speech therapy & other memory loss improvement methods…............…. 127

Subchapter VI-5. Fears 130
Family One: Bob (the radio announcer) and Kay…. 130
Family Two: Clay (the CEO) and Pam…............... 131

Family Three: Sarah & Eve (mother/daughter team)133
Family Four: Steve (pilot/executive) & Laura........ 135
Reflections on fears ....…................... 135

Subchapter VI-6
*Family living arrangements, adjustments,
situations, and behaviors of children* ....…... 136
Family One: Bob (the radio announcer) and Kay..... 136
Family Two: Clay (the CEO) and Pam..………….. 139
Family Three: Sarah & Eve (mother/daughter team) 142
Family Four: Steve (pilot/executive) & Laura…….. 144
Reflections on families' post memory loss living
arrangements, situations, & responses of children 144

Subchapters VI-7
*Role reversals & changes affecting family
dynamics* ....……. 146
Family One: Bob (the radio announcer) and Kay... 146
Family Two: Clay (the CEO) and Pam 147
Family Three: Sarah & Eve (mother/daughter team) 149
Family Four: Steve (pilot/executive) & Laura…….. 151
Reflections on role reversals and changes
affecting family dynamics………………………….. 152

Subchapter VI-8
Marriage relationship losses.......................….. 153
Family One: Bob (the radio announcer) and Kay….. 153
Family Two: Clay (the CEO) Pam..……………..… 155
Family Three: Sarah & Eve(mother/daughter team) 157
Family Four: Steve (pilot/executive) & Laura…….. 158
Reflections on marriage relationship losses…….… 159

Subchapter VI-9
Life style losses—Personality, social, financial, and career-related... 161
Family One: Bob (the radio announcer) and Kay..... 161
Family Two: Clay (the CEO) and Pam................. 162
Family Three: Sarah & Eve (mother/daughter team) 166
Family Four: Steve (pilot/executive) & Laura......... 167
Reflections: Personality, social, financial, & career-related 170

Subchapter VI-10
Outside and professional health care and psycho-therapeutic support............................. 171
Family One: Bob (the radio announcer) and Kay..... 171
Family Two: Clay (the CEO) and Pam................. 173
Family Three: Sarah & Eve (mother/daughter team) 177
Family Four: Steve (pilot/executive) & Laura......... 180
Reflections: Outside/professional health care & psychotherapeutic support................................ 182

Subchapter VI-11
Coping and psychological manifestations 186
Family One: Bob (the radio announcer) and Kay..... 186
Family Two: Clay (the CEO) and Pam................. 188
Family Three: Sarah & Eve (mother/daughter team) 189
Family Four: Steve (pilot/executive) & Laura......... 192
Reflections on coping & psychological manifestations 193

**Chapter VII: Amazing Stories—
"To Do" and "Not To Do"**............................. 195
Tina's Head Injury—
You Can't Believe Everything You Hear............. 195
A Neurologist's Examination 197
Being in the Positive Present Moment.................. 199
Being Shut Down.. 199
Reacting to Forgetting..................................... 200
Danny's Accident and Working as a Team........... 200
Working Out—Exercising the Mind....................201
A Family Who Couldn't Afford Therapy.............. 202
A Family Project..202
The Beginning 203
Six Years Later.. 203
Failure through Criticism and Attitude................. 204
<u>Regarding Henry</u> vs. <u>Memento</u>......................... 205
Without Laura's Support................................... 205
Love Saved Danny.. 206
The Difficulties of an Emotional Aphasia 207
Hopefulness and Grieving................................. 208
Depression.. 208
To Speak or Not to Speak................................. 209
Negative Therapy Reports Can
Interfere with Your Benefits............................. 210
Plan.. 211
Sing Songs and Read Audio Books Aloud............. 213
Pick Appropriate Materials................................214
Support Groups..215
Body Language.. 215
You—the Default Healer.................................. 216
If You Think You Can't You're Right—

xiv

If You Think You Can You're Right.................217
Final Note.................…..........................218

Part Three... 220
Appendix A: Memory Loss Glossary 221
    Aphasia.. 221
    Receptive Aphasia............................... 221
    Agnosia... 222
    Dysgnosia..222
    Expressive aphasias............................ 222
    Anomia...223
    Dysnomia... 223
    Apraxia and Dysarthria........................ 224
    Alexia...224
    Dyslexia... 224
    Acalculia.. 225
    Agraphia/Dysgraphia........................... 225
    Agrammatism...................................... 225
    Astereognosis......................................225
    Dysstereognosis.................................. 226
    Dementia.. 226
    Aphasia associated deficits................... 226
    Jargon.. 226
    Neologisms.. 226
    Paraphasias..226
    Perseveration.....................................226

Appendix B: Different Types of Serious Memory
Loss affecting Language Memory...................... 227

Appendix C: Treatment and Internet Resources for Memory-Training, Treatment Books, Support Groups, and Memory Loss Plans........................... 231

Appendix D: 25 Tips for Serious Memory Loss and Memory-training....................................... 235

Appendix E: RDA/ Minimum Vitamins and Minerals compare to Wheat Grass...................... 244

<u>Memory Support Health Food Shopping List</u>..... 248

Bibliography... 249

Index.. 268

Contact the Author... 273

Introduction

Memory loss and forgotten words are traumatic for anybody, instantly changing lives and futures. But pause and consider these true stories: Bob was a radio manager who lost his memory of many words, and thus, his quick tongue, but still managed and continued to run his radio station afterwards. Clay was a furniture storeowner, who couldn't remember one word, but eventually, relearned them all with the help of his wife and children. Tina believed a hopeless diagnosis that she would lose her remaining memory and abilities completely, and sent her new husband away in despair. Only later, did she begin a new healthy life and resume her former career as a music teacher, which requires good memory. Steve's wife insisted on therapy for him, and he has been improving, remembering, and communicating better for over fourteen years, instead of being placed in the home suggested by his doctor. Danny's family found great satisfaction in helping him learn to think and remember again after head injury in spite of his memory loss. Now he lives and works on his own. My own mother had normal age-associated memory loss problems a few years ago and now, they seldom appear.

How do these improvements happen? How do people go on and regain lost memory, cognition, communication, and the ability to function in society again? For one thing, they and their families develop a healing attitude necessary to go on and get well. They allow the persons with memory loss to become "students" regaining memory, rather than "disabled" persons. In my clinical experiences working with memory loss associated with serious disorders for over 20 years, this mindset, which involves a positive attitude and learning about memory loss is probably the most important element in restoring it. This healthy thought process needed for recovery requires awareness, support, and education. In the end, memory loss improvement comes best with some encouragement; the kind one would give a student learning a musical instrument or a foreign language. However, as far as the actual study requirements for the memory loss student—they're not that hard—rehearsing a few basics everyday is all there is to it and then resuming one's favorite mental activities. These are all normal activities of daily life anyway. If memory and mental exercise are not part of one's every day routine already, this will increase memory decline. There is truth in the saying "use it or lose it" for everyone when it comes to memory.

When memory loss recovery is due to illness, believe me, this encouraging attitude I speak of is not divvied out exclusively to therapists. Actually, families who want the best for each other already have more of the right stuff than any therapist. Think about it. How many school children from families who care will be asked to study tonight? Similarly, how many babies do you know of who won't be encouraged by their families to walk and talk this year? Your average baby will be encouraged until he does walk and talk in a good family. Could that be the reason that they do learn and walk and talk? Isn't it true that without someone who cares standing by, both the baby and the school child could easily fail? Could it be that encouragement may be something we all need at many points throughout our lives, even our elderly lives? Could we be letting go of our elderly before we should because of a much larger agenda we do not control? We need to think about this as a society and what it means.

When memory loss becomes a problem in those we love and want to help, many people step up to the plate easily to help with the same manner of giving and receiving necessary for everyone throughout all of life. However, in today's world, we like the quick fix best. In this world of medicines and high tech health care, we believe that rapid answers will come. Everyone's waiting for that new drug miracle even though we have many of the answers already! In recovery after serious memory loss disease, the nervous system may not be quick to respond, but with an expectant, encouraging attitude and a healthy environment high in specific nutrition, mild exercise, routine mental challenge, and low stress, it proceeds at a much faster pace. Under these circumstances, even people originally not expected to improve much, can do so dramatically and spontaneously.

However, not everyone's case is the same, so let's think for a minute—what is normal for human memory? Children take about 12 years to get a good education. Some move more quickly, some more slowly, and some rarely study and learn plenty anyway because of a naturally good memory. Others will study everything, and still crave more throughout their lifetimes building a strong memory as they proceed. Babies will go on taking about a year or two before they walk and talk developing language and motor memory as they go. The point: Memories, language, and skilled learning are unique to each of us, yet they develop over a reasonable amount of time, not in a major hurry. They heal the same way. Just like broken legs and arms, damaged brain tissues respond over certain time frames. Fortunately, science research is finally catching up and reporting that brain cells do heal.

So, could someone's memory return in a speedy way? Sometimes, but other times it takes a fairly long time. No one knows the answer in each case for sure. Therein lies the problem. Unfortunately, some families feel very hopeless after talking to professionals when memory loss occurs, as though it cannot be improved at all. That's not true, but when families hear that no one knows for sure, often they tend to take that to mean cure is impossible or practically so. Of course, this belief alone and the attitude it carries with it, that there is 'no cure' will destroy any chances for memory loss recovery with serious illness. Once memory loss families give up, all recovery bets are off! Learn the facts shared by the survivors in part two of this book. Many people who don't give up succeed and have proven—*memory loss can be healed, and if so—memory loss must be healed*—to maintain quality of life.

When memory loss rehabilitation is not attempted, a horrible hopelessness seems to set in: That of sitting by and almost waiting for death to occur. This is destructive and could only be tolerated out of ignorance. If recovery attempts are really no harder than encouraging a school child and eating certain healthy foods, what do we have to lose? Do we need proof of what will occur before we can begin to expect improvements that could come if we do the right thing? Healing is the norm in every area of the body properly treated. Someday this could be your own memory loss problem! Yes, I say that because memory loss is presently at an all time high and on the rise because of our aging population.

In essence, memory loss healing happens best and most rapidly when we learn about the problem, study the solutions, and then believe, expect, encourage, and continue to do our best no matter where the road may *appear* to be leading. Remember, the act of attempting recovery even in a diseased memory is always for the good of all involved regardless of whether there is a perfect final outcome.

Those Who Care—Can

Before we begin, I take my hat off to those of you who have the courage to learn about helping someone you care about in a time when the love of learning has nearly faded and the compassion to be there is priceless. It takes courage to help someone you care about especially if you are going through that awfully difficult period of adjusting to the illness that caused all this. Remember, it has always taken courage to do anything of lasting value. Only those like you reading this, who care—can. Your desire to learn about the proper handling of memory loss is truly a gift to yourself and the person you are helping.

Part One

Chapter 1

Causes of Memory Loss—
What's in a Name?

Chapter 2

Anti-Aging and
Overlooked Memory Losses

Chapter 3

The Keep It Simple—
Facts of Serious Memory Loss

Chapter 4

Like the Traveling Language Student

Chapter One

Causes of Memory Loss—What's in a Name?

Let's start by talking about a concern for those with the major forms of memory loss problems: Understanding the difference between memory loss for language and other memory losses like forgetfulness, confusion or the inability to put ideas together. Most people may understand that sudden difficulty in recalling thoughts, words or ideas is usually due to some injury brought on by the lack of oxygen to the brain's blood supply. Someone who loses basic vocabulary words may then be labeled as having the disorder called "aphasia," the most common form of memory loss, which mainly involves language memory. Here you will be introduced to aphasia with more descriptive terms like, "word loss, forgotten language, or language memory loss, etc." However, understand that other forms of memory loss; similar to what we see in Alzheimer's, often occur when people have language memory loss. For example, those with head injury or stroke often have language memory loss, but may also show signs of: disorientation, forgetfulness of things and people, mixing up events in time, spatial disorientation, repetitiveness, difficulties with clear thinking, emotional problems and social withdrawal. Usually, these problems, like forgetting what just happened a moment ago or yesterday, will be a greater problem for those with Alzheimer's.

DON'T FORGET

Memory Loss Diagnosis

The American Psychiatric Association (APA) is the organization, which created the diagnoses for memory loss disorders, all found under the broad umbrella of *"dementias"* in their manual, *the Diagnostic and Statistical Manual-IV-TR* (DSM-IV-TR). So what is *dementia* then, and why is that a concern for those with memory loss? *Dementia* is the term currently used to cover all intellectual and cognitive loss, and also, the term implies an inability to relearn. Memory loss of language after stroke or head injury can usually be relearned in time, and yet, this type of memory loss still remains under the general *dementia* headings. Only in the past year, have insurance companies begun to recognize that loss as correctable once again. Of course, therapists have known and lobbied about this for years. Frankly, it only became a problem since managed care took over insurance.

Memory Loss Therapy After Stroke or Head-Injury

Since memory loss after stroke or head injury can often be totally healed or at least significantly diminished, these therapies have been going on for many decades. Unfortunately, when the wrong *dementia* term was used, treatments allowed by insurers for the different types of memory loss got confused. Alzheimer's *dementia* was often mixed up with stroke or head injury *dementia* diagnoses as all of them are labeled *dementia*. Insurers paid for the stroke or head injury therapy until the *dementia* confusions began to make problems. This form of therapy is memory-training or language therapy usually called speech therapy. Memory of specific people, places, events, spatial

CHAPTER ONE   JOYCE

orientation, thinking, and lost vocabulary, reading, writing, and grammar is what speech therapy retrains with plenty of success I might add. Thus, permanent memory loss after stroke or head injury is not the rule.

Memory Loss Therapy After Alzheimer's

Helping to remedy this situation, today more and more reports of improvement from early Alzheimer's are coming out of the research in persons who receive similar memory-training to the type done in the past only for stroke, head-injury, or other memory losses (Clare, 2002). Even moderate and severe Alzheimer's cases are responding favorably to the memory-training. Hopefully, this new research will impact therapy for all problems under the *dementia* heading. Insurance companies will not be able to point to *dementias* and claim nothing can be done when the most serious memory loss problem we have on the planet is responding to this help. Certainly, this should improve receipt of therapy benefits in problems known to be more correctable such as stroke or head injury. If Alzheimer's people get help, definitely stroke and head injury must be better cared for now also! Unfortunately, that has not been the case in this insurance climate.

Though memory-training/speech therapy is not a cure, so far, it has proven helpful to Alzheimer's showing this type of mental activity will improve early cases, and support and prevent further declines during mid and late stages. An Alzheimer's program should offer: Recall of specific people, places, events, spatial orientation, organization, memory chunking, thinking, cognition and lost vocabulary, reading, writing, and grammar.

DON'T FORGET

Alzheimer's or Age-Associated Memory Loss?

Now more than ever, these healing reports keep coming for those with early Alzheimer's, just by doing memory-training and things that have been around for a long time. So don't give up—do what you can now! Remember, not everyone who thinks they are on the road to Alzheimer's truly is anyway! Making that assumption could be a real mistake. Many suffer age-associated memory impairments (AAMI), which can be stalled in their tracks by memory nutrition and phosphatidylserine from your local health food store (Crook & Adderly, 1998). Simple truths like these and others I will share, already known about prevention of memory loss are not being put to good use.

Inappropriateness of Dementia Label

My main concern in differentiating the *dementia* labels for you here is to offer all memory loss persons the correct and complete therapy available through their insurance carrier. Therefore, when mild language memory loss from stroke or head injury is the only problem, I do not favor the pejorative term *"dementia,"* which is losing its steam in light of all the research. *Dementia* implies many things including that the person may have trouble relearning. This is now proven to be untrue. However, the medical world we rely upon seems to be stuck with *dementia* as an overarching label used whenever memory loss is present, repairable or not. The term is just so insulting, don't you think? Would you feel like studying or expect to get well if you discovered you had a diagnosis of *dementia?* Maybe we could dump the term altogether and

CHAPTER ONE   J O Y C E

affectionately call it the *senior dip*. Maybe we could give up the assumptions that these memory problems are incurable at the same time! Changing that term would help.

Need to Know Diagnostic Classifications

When memory loss is due to a *stroke*, your doctor may call it *vascular dementia,* or *multi-infarct dementia.* When *head injury* is the cause there may also be *amnesia*. Head injuries are called *dementias due to general medical conditions.* These categories are vital to know to receive proper treatment and benefits in memory loss cases. Your medical doctor will prescribe medications for both stroke and Alzheimer's to increase mental acuity and aid in maximizing recovery during memory-training programs or during your own home memory-training plan. These medications are especially helpful when the Alzheimer's is detected early on.

Start the Mental Exercises

If for any reason, your medical professionals are not offering cognitive retraining, then go ahead and try personal homework, mental exercises or memory-training plans of your own. With this book and its references (Appendix C & D) as a guide, ask a speech therapist, memory trainer, or even an interested teacher to help you decide where to begin. The training will exercise and protect the existing mental acuity. Alzheimer's should be handled with the same positive healing attitude, acceptance, and encouragement as the other memory loss disorders. This triad of support acts as a big preventative to other problems and is part of the ongoing recovery. If you cannot afford therapists to help or begin mental exercises that seem appropriate, look for group memory-training sites for the elderly usually handled by trained nurses or adult day care centers. All memory loss support groups and memory-training plans will be invaluable.

Informing or Not Informing Families of the Nature of the Memory Loss

So, back at the hospital where the strokes and head injuries started, you might be thinking, 'What's to tell about memory loss?' Maybe you're thinking the whole memory loss thing is just an obvious issue that can't be helped. Wrong. A major problem with memory loss is that though it is very well documented and thoroughly researched, medical professionals often do not send patients home from the hospital with many facts about what to do when it happens.

For example, many of the families in part two of this book had language memory loss, which needs attention after the hospitalization, but their families did not learn anything about the memory losses during their hospital stays. Most of the people had to learn about language memory loss and its symptoms on their own after the hospitalization. One of the stroke victims researched the disorder himself before he got well. This shows that his mind was still working regardless of the impairment. The other persons were devoted to telling their stories to anyone who would listen. They wanted to teach people that they could get well if they followed a few guidelines.

CHAPTER ONE **JOYCE**

Consequences of Not Informing

After stroke or head injury, it is important to begin services as soon as possible or else to begin to have the persons study on their own to get the best results. Language memory loss responds most favorably during the first year or so of the healing phase. That is considered to be the window of maximum opportunity. However, many families do not learn about this during the hospital stay or to expect that some cases are really stubborn, and can look truly devastating. Nor do they learn, attention to therapy, some simple word exercises, and home study is needed, and that these activities reduce stress, helping the situation, not hurting it. Nor do they learn that often those same tough cases make surprising turns when they practice this way. I have seen them recover completely time and again. Nor do families learn what I have shared with you: Research now corroborates, the brain heals after all (Rossi, 2002). This is something therapists in the trenches have known all along. Of course, for this healing to happen, people need a bit of this lacking information.

The State of Our Nation's Hospitals--Memory Loss Protocol

So what do patients and families learn at the hospital if there is a memory loss? Either they stay in the hospital long enough to receive a dribble of therapy from a speech therapist, or they are simply told to go home and call one. They are sometimes told the person will never speak again and will get progressively more confused and deteriorate. Hopefully, they are not so devastated and worried sick about the person's weakened state that they will forget to call for the therapeutic help within the time frame an insurance carrier will require them to. Hopefully, they will have the name and number of a therapist to call from the hospital. Hopefully, the person responsible is not an ailing elderly spouse already enormously overwhelmed.

My fourth desire is: Why doesn't the therapist follow the person instead of the family being required to call or search for one? Of course I know why. This was protocol in years gone by before managed care. I'm sure medical professionals still want that to be in effect, but they are not in charge. Insurance companies are! So much for twenty-first century health-care improvements.

Hard Realities and Reasons for Hope

Other important facts that the DSM-IV-TR reveals about the language memory losses are that they cause significant social and occupational changes and a serious decline in communication due to the forgotten and lost vocabulary. Let's face it, especially in the beginning, expect a challenge. Though loss of language memory can be mild to severe, the results are often devastating at least for a time. The effects on family members are intense and include touchy emotions and intimacy challenges. Life is not going to be exactly the same, but many people do overcome. Some people, like the people you will meet in part two of this book, were totally cured.

Family Involvement

Once spouses and family members recognize that the possibility of improvement is so high if treated

CHAPTER ONE   J OYCE

properly, they usually respond to the needs of the healing process and assist in efforts to reclaim the loss of memory and lost communication skills. Frankly, the need for family and friends to become aware and help in whatever way they can has greatly increased since medical benefits have become so rationed out and costly that doctors must decide whether the persons will walk, use their hands, or regain memory, think and talk again, by prescribing the specific therapy regimen. *Essentially, the family and friends have become the default healers for those areas left untreated.* Unfortunately, without family and caregiver understanding, encouragement and patience, the declines and memory losses will more than likely remain.

Critical Need for Education, Awareness, Solutions

Please understand that most doctors and hospitals attempt to properly inform patients and families of their options to the best of their ability. Patients and families are often highly stressed at these times, and unfortunately, may misunderstand the importance of action. Some hospitals appear less able to properly inform, as was the case in my research, and as I hear from people every day who have suffered similar memory loss problems that affect speaking and thinking abilities. This lack of education for families or caregivers happens for many reasons. Some professionals fear that the family is too overwhelmed to accept the information at the time of an accident or stroke and should not be burdened initially. I fear that this mentality takes the risk of losing the person with the language memory loss and allows them to fall through the ever-widening cracks in the health care system. In addition, as a psychotherapist and speech therapist, I have seen a huge decline in language memory loss treatment since the advent of managed care, which allocates only minimal funding for memory and communication rehabilitation. Memory loss is now becoming a major problem in this generation of U.S. history due to the increased amount of elderly people.

In my opinion, the need for education, awareness, and solutions are at critical levels for both long-term memory loss exemplified by language memory loss, widespread in memory impairments, and short-term, recent memory loss, which occurs the most in early Alzheimer's. Latter stages of Alzheimer's contain both short and long-term memory loss.

Chapter Two

Anti-Aging and Overlooked Memory Losses

Save Your Brain with an Ounce of Prevention—the Anti-Aging Regimen

For those of us, who still have our memories, or others, who are showing signs of age-associated memory impairments (AAMI), we must begin now to improve and protect our aging memories right along with the memories of our parents and friends. First, let me assure you, what I said already holds true, daily mental exercise is a must. Next, you must get oxygen and nutrition to the brain. So exercise, walk, or use a treadmill, but do something physical daily. Even short walks, morning and evening, have proven to increase longevity and decrease stress at the same time. Stress is toxic to the memory. Use any other forms of stress reduction that help you also: Music is known to enhance memory. Art, dance, prayer, spiritual meditation, or use of special talents or gifts are all very helpful to those who choose them.

A Digestible Basic for Memory Health

One of the easiest and most inexpensive ways to get the basic daily nutrition necessary for healthy memory is by taking wheat grass, 3-6 tablespoons, more or less, depending upon individual need and the potency of the wheat grass product. This is a whole food, not a vitamin, taken throughout the day and packed with many essential memory nutrients: Vitamin B complex, folic acid, E, A, C, choline, zinc, magnesium, selenium, tryptophan,

DON'T FORGET

glutamine, and tyrosine.

PS / Vital to the Prescription

Also, of extreme importance, go to your local health food store and ask for phosphatidylserine (PS). Take 100 milligrams three times per day. PS is best taken mixed with phosphatidylcholine (PC) or lecithin, both are forms of choline, and make up the fluid of our brain, acetylcholine. These choline derivatives boost PS, an important natural substance our bodies produce, which decreases as we age, but sends information to the memory center of our brain called the hippocampus through the brain fluid, acetylcholine. PS has been used in Italy and other parts of Europe for years and has been tested thoroughly and found to be extremely effective in prevention of memory loss (Kidd, 1998). Take it regularly with vitamins E, B and omega 3 oil (Appendix E, p. 148).

Diet and Valuable Memory Enhancements

Experiment with the numerous other incredible natural memory loss preventatives that rejuvenate aging memories: Vinpocetine, huperzine A, bacopa monniera, galantamine, carnosine, COQ10, acetyl-L-carnitine, alpha lipoic acid, and inositol (See Appendix E). Other herbs and supplements, which boost PS effectiveness, include ginseng and ginkgo biloba. If you took gingko in the past and it did not help, you needed PS first to gas the engine. DHEA, pregnenolone, ginseng, and ginkgo also help menopausal memory lags. Hormone replacement therapy (HRT) is necessary, but learn about the safer, natural cream and supplement versions. Also, use aspirin or ibuprofen regularly for any inflammation, which is harmful to aging brains.

Finally, eat a memory nutritious diet of anti-oxidizing berries and fruits; eggs, fish, walnuts, almonds, and avocadoes; plenty of leafy greens, and also, low carbohydrate veggies like onions, spinach, cauliflower, and asparagus. Cook safely, using olive oil or real butter.

Water and Juicing

Be very sure to add plenty of spring or distilled water to your day. If you can't seem to get 8-12 glasses in easily, here are a few tricks. Add good water to any real juice you normally drink saving money and reducing high caloric intake that is not good for your brain. Mixing a bit of apple or cranberry juice with water works well. Put lots of anti-oxidant green tea and decaffeinated herbal teas into your life. Mixed with a touch of lemon or lemonade, they can taste just like old-fashioned iced tea from my grandmother's kitchen. Also add a lemon or lime to your water or buy some of the great tasting waters available today. Avoid sodas or sugary grocery store juice products! Sugar does not help the health of the brain. Never go to bed without water or a fluid to sip by your bedside to refresh your palate if you awaken thirsty. Carry bottles of fresh water with you in your car. A sip here, a sip there; make it a habit to keep yourself hydrated.

Wheat grass is solidly loaded with brain nutrition, and is the main healing product you should be drinking in fresh juices. However, there are many people learning about helpful juices of other kinds for anti-aging. You can learn about the art of juicing raw fruits and vegetables on the Internet (www.mercola.com) and read on for recipes.

DON'T FORGET

Mercury and Aluminum Toxins

Vary your fish choices due to reports of high mercury levels at this time. Avoid swordfish, shark, tilefish, and king mackerel. Large predatory fish are the most suspect. Choose the ocean varieties of fish such as ocean salmon and sardines rather than those raised in fresh water. Check mercury levels in your local buying area by calling 1-800-SAFEFOOD. Even tuna has reports of increased mercury with recommendations to reduce consumption to once per week in some areas. Shellfish is also a viable alternative. Some researchers are so concerned about mercury; they suggest removal of mercury dental fillings if possible over time.

Keep up with the research on aluminum found in antacids, artificial creamers, deodorants, treated water and enhanced by fluoride. No one wants to commit to totally abandoning metal cookware with aluminum yet, but there's plenty of talk about the possibility in the future. Many people have already found aluminum free brands.

Anesthesia, Drugs, and Alcohol

Anesthesia, drugs, and alcohol are also offenders of memory creating some serious memory loss problems. Korsakoff's syndrome, caused by heavy alcohol intake, creates amnesias and is one of the worst forms of memory loss known to man! Consider drugs and alcohol toxic to your system knowing research shows more than four drinks per week increase cognitive memory losses. Complete abstinence is not necessary; unless you drink alcohol the way some people eat potato chips. Remember the ad? "Bet you can't eat just one." Can you drink just the four permitted alcoholic drinks per week? Red wine is the one healthy choice, but only if you can follow these guidelines: Six-eight ounces, no more than every other day. Otherwise, it would be better to abstain. Regular alcohol intake removes nutrients and vitamins. Aging brains and sensitive ones do not fair well with such toxins.

Cigarettes

Cigarette smokers also show decreased memory abilities in studies and seem to light up the most in response to depression and anxiety also harmful to the memory. When they do, the cadmium content in the cigarettes destroys Vitamins C, B, E, selenium, and zinc, all vital to healthy memory (Crook & Adderly, 1998). Although there may appear to be a moment of clarity, comfort, and reduced anxiety from the nicotine, which does boast a memory neurotransmitter site, the long-term damage to memory is the problem. Truthfully, as with most habit-forming substances, cigarettes tell a tale of socially accepted self-medication that perpetuates itself. Use of wheat grass and other nutrients, can detoxify the system and decrease urges by filling real health needs, thus making it much easier to quit. So I highly recommend wheat grass cleansing to smokers, as it destroys cravings without causing withdrawal.

Coffee

I was an avid coffee drinker when I started taking wheat grass. My interest in coffee disappeared without headaches or the slightest desire. I simply forgot about it because my needs were being met elsewhere. I had no intention of quitting. However, caffeine increases insulin and fat storage and is also a vasoconstrictor limiting brain activity after the initial jolt. Small amounts like one cup per day are not problematic. Green antioxidant tea is a good substitute with healing properties for a person avoiding memory loss. Wheat grass will give incredible morning energy eliminating any desire for caffeine.

Benzodiazepines, Prozac and Legal Drugs

Obviously, other more serious drugs, both legal and illegal affect memory. The family of drugs known as benzodiazepines is particularly hard on the elderly. Seniors who have used them at length report memory abilities similar to people suffering from serious chronic medical conditions (Crook & Adderly, 1998). Prozac creates its own world of problems from manic episodes and lack of empathy to loss of short and long-term memory. There are so many better ways to assist depression by healing the memory center of the brain that don't have people running to survival groups afterwards (Null, 2000). When you heal your memory, you also heal your emotions.

A word of caution is in order: Slowly wean from any serious drugs with assistance from a nutrition conscious doctor if possible. Dependency and addictions develop, withdrawal can be difficult, and a weaning process is necessary. Cleanse and detoxify on the wheat grass while weaning under your doctor's direction. He or she may know nothing of wheat grass or memory nutrition, but you must be slowly removed from these substances with medical help. Maybe your psychiatrist will help you wean, but not all of them will want to advise their patients toward independent functioning. Call around until you find a doctor who agrees you can become healthy without the addictive chemicals.

Marijuana

SPECT brain studies also show decreased activity in the pre-frontal cortex and the temporal lobes of marijuana users. Abnormal activity in the temporal lobes is associated with problems in memory, learning, and motivation. Users for more than a year often fail in learning due to amotivational syndrome and drop out of learning environments (Amen, 1998). Detoxification with wheat grass and nutrients even makes a dent in regular marijuana use. Once one feels so good after taking wheat grass, PS, PC and vitamin E, it becomes rather ridiculous to destroy all the vital nutrients that have been missing by smoking weed.

Anger, Anxiety, Stress, and Depression

Simple anxiety, stress, and depression create a hormone called cortisol, which attacks the hippocampus memory center of the brain. When you're overly stressed or stimulated, you often can't think straight, right? Avoid cortisol. Anger elevates cortisol for up to six hours, whereas meditation and prayer reduce it (Null, 2000). This is how our normal body chemistry works. Remember the nutrients we have discussed here in the wheat grass assist memory located in the brain. Any vitamins that assist memory also decrease anxiety and depression. The PS also has a great record for reducing depression as well

DON'T FORGET

as increasing memory, as do the other vitamins mentioned. In the evening, if you do need a calming herb, pick kava kava, valarian, or chamomile. Even highly needed calcium, vital to the elderly skeletal system, is known to calm nerves and is therefore of assistance to the memory process always hindered by anxiety and stress.

Reasons for Wheat Grass

The contents of the wheat grass are charted in Appendix E along with the vital list of memory nutrients. Though wheat grass is not classified as a vitamin, but as a whole food, the nutrients of 15 pounds equal those of 350 pounds of fresh, choice vegetables. The wheat grass boasts cleansing qualities important for any person having difficulty giving up habit-forming substances. Even persons who have only experienced the toxicity of depression need this cleansing regimen as a start to memory health.

Drug Companies

Remember prescription drugs treat symptoms. Preventing the underlying cause with health and cleansing is the much wiser approach with a much better result. This is possible for the memory problems described here and especially for age-associated memory impairment (AAMI). People all over this country are finally realizing that nutrition is probably the most important part of our healthcare, and this is no less true for memory loss. $37 billion went to natural and organic foods and dietary supplements in the U.S. last year (www.Mercola.com).

CHAPTER TWO   JOYCE

    Drug companies are paying big bucks as our country learns to cut down on medical and insurance costs by turning to natural alternatives. They have learned what we are learning—a holistic approach that includes nutrition and vitamin supplements is vital to healing, and it seems they're not very happy about it. You see, no drug alone can do all the healing for mild or serious illnesses. We still need to live properly. The drugs take care of symptoms. They may allow us to be more comfortable, think, and behave better artificially for a time, but our nutrition and way of life offers us an independent stability and health that will not create other problems later. In the end, memory and mental health require these nutrients regardless of the drugs taken or the cures on the way from pharmaceutical sources. We may as well get with it and care for ourselves.

    Because of these changes and lost profits, there is a battle on now for vitamin regulation. Look at the Dietary Supplement Safety Act of 2003. If it passes vitamin prices will rise. Many are already difficult to get in other countries. Here in the U.S., it seems leading pharmaceutical companies are paying for research to discredit natural remedies. If drug companies continue, vitamins could become impossible to purchase over the counter. That's another reason I want to get the word out about wheat grass. As a whole food, it will not likely be easily regulated and is available at health food stores, whole food grocery stores, and at my website.

    Sadly, drug companies do not want their profits torn asunder by the likes of St. John's Wart, for example, which hurt Pfizer's Prozac sales. Pfizer launched a study to prove the lack of efficacy of the herb to save their sales and discredit—a vitamin product! Plenty of drugs need a closer look. So why aren't they launching research to protect people from benzodiazepine addiction, or the 100,000 deaths per year from prescription drugs? Their own house is the one in disrepair. Why would they concern themselves with something as insignificant as vitamin over-dosages when their own products are doing so much damage and as a whole, vitamins are as necessary as water, air, and food?

Drugs and vitamins are not the same though some would like us to believe they are. Others would like government regulation of vitamins, which would only compound our problems and invite pharmaceutical companies in to take them over. Drug companies have proven, they are no more interested in helping you find wheat grass, phosphatidylserine/PS, choline, vinpocetine, huperzine A, or galantamine, which enhance the memory naturally. As usual, it's all about dollars and cents! They have their own interests at heart! So who's going to tell you about these nutrients? I hope we all start telling each other and learn the many medicinal qualities of food!

My Mom's Age Associated Memory Loss

My knowledge about this increased when my own 81-year old mother opted to work on her memory loss a few years ago after feeling depressed about my father's death. By the way, that's all it takes is an adjustment that is depressing or stressful. When elderly people stop eating and sleeping properly and are upset, the memory will suffer. Though I had worked with serious memory loss throughout my career, I had few ideas about nutrition and memory loss prevention when we started other than regular use of vitamin E and aspirin. My mother always exercised her mind and body, but her depression was cutting back on her desire for even those forms of activity.

So we started researching as everyone does, and found basic memory nutrients like B complex, folic acid, C, zinc, and Vitamin E. Later, we added COQ10, alpha lipoic acid, choline/lecithin, inositol, l-tyrosine, l-glutamine, DHEA, and omega 3 oils capsules. She was very faithful and ate green leafy and other vegetables, fruits, soy proteins, fish, eggs, and other whole foods, as well. We cut out processed foods for the most part and reduced processed carbohydrates, especially ones mixed with heavy fats. She continued to like soy products and ate those regularly. She felt pretty good. However, this involved swallowing and trying to absorb numerous vitamins everyday. She opted to take them throughout the day as she ate, but the process was nothing to write home about and sometimes upset her stomach. However, her memory did improve.

Later, I thought we found an easier solution, in a program of memory vitamins to take in the morning and evening similar to ones I find in health food stores. She took those for a month and said they were not nearly as potent as what we had done before. Obviously, the potency you settle on should be based on your own body and the guidelines in Appendix E. She decided she would go back to taking handfuls of vitamins everyday.

Wheat Grass, PS, and Tony Robbins

Then we fell upon the wheat grass this past year and phosphatydlserine (PS). Actually, I was taking it on a recommendation from Tony Robbins (2000), the life

DON'T FORGET

coach out there offering people extraordinary lives. When mom tried it, she couldn't believe the energy and clarity it gave her starting from the very first day. Plus, taken in the liquid form, the nutrients seemed to absorb almost immediately in her elderly body. Plus, she could swallow the additional supplements down more easily with the wheat grass mixture. Since she is very healthy, she started out immediately taking about three tablespoons a day. Not everyone can do that. Persons who have been ill may be overly toxic and need to start slower, perhaps taking 1-2 tablespoons for the first few days building up to more.

Recipes

In our drinks, we often add a bit of soy or whey protein powder to the blender with the three tablespoons of wheat grass. Usually, we start with frozen fruits and berries from the freezer section of the supermarket to create more of a breakfast drink. Into fruit or ice, we blend 8-16 fluid ounces of water, real juice, or green tea, which boasts memory-fighting anti-oxidants. You can easily swallow down the phosphatidyserine/PS, Vitamin E and other vitamins with your drink. Sometimes I drink it all at one sitting. Other times I make a blender full and save half in the refrigerator to drink before lunch or with a four PM snack adding two more PS capsules before the day is gone. Some days, my mother puts her wheat grass in other foods like eggs, salads, or soups. I've mixed it with an ounce or two of water in a small glass and then chased it down with something else. The point is—take it! We rarely take it at night—with so many vitamins. Try to get your last dose in by five PM or just drink two earlier in the day. Though it can look a bit funny and awfully

CHAPTER TWO — JOYCE

green, it reminds me of green liquid applesauce now that I'm used to it. The thickness of it really helps with ingestion of the other memory vitamins. No more nausea!

This process began saving us quite a bit of money since the wheat grass contains so many of the other needed vitamins that we were buying separately before. Now the extra vitamins we buy from the memory list are minimal compared to what we were doing. We never forget the PS, a choline product, or extra Vitamin E. Plus, we still get COQ10 and alpha lipoic acid. Her memory has really become top notch again for her age. The memory problems she had at age 78-79 have all but disappeared. To me, this is truly amazing after watching her closely for several years.

People with memory loss, need to put up reminders or write themselves notes to get started on this nutrition. Get in the habit early in the morning or sip wheat grass drinks throughout your day taking PS also. The day will go more smoothly if you develop a ritual.

While wheat grass removes toxins and has cleansing qualities that heal, it is not like taking fiber. The fruit adds fiber or you could choose to mix some powder fiber into the drink now and then or have fiber separately. However, start slowly if you have not been well. And don't encourage pregnant women to take it, as the baby may receive the toxins being cleansed out of the body in the breast milk. If you are on medications, share the list of nutrients found in wheat grass listed in Appendix E with your doctor.

Vitamins and Coumadin—What We Did

After a hip surgery, my mom was asked to stop

DON'T FORGET

the vitamins and just take coumadin as many of you with serious illnesses have had to do. However, a month after the surgery, she asked her doctors to please allow her to go off the coumadin so she could return to her healthy eating style which made her feel and think much better. Not everyone could do this, as you will learn in part two, but fact was, she felt better on the healthy diet. Her doctor permitted this, but wanted to be sure she kept up her equally powerful vitamin program. So truly, her food and vitamins are now her medicine, in more ways than one.

Waiting for the Cure

For those of you simply waiting for a magic pill, drug cures may come, but they might not. If you wait and don't keep your memory up to the best levels you can, you may be in for a sad state of affairs. Please don't expect your answers from the drug companies!

In my practice, time and time again, I see people held back by serious medications they become dependent upon. Eventually there is a problem, a reason they can't take them anymore, a reaction to something else, or an interference from other health issues or the medicines of another disorder. Sometimes, the medicines just make them act weird or feel funny. Eventually, they take their toll. Many healthy things people could have done are put to the side. Don't let this happen to you! Decide to work on memory loss prevention if you have not begun to suffer from serious illness requiring medications that contraindicate this program.

In the future, I believe we will learn how to eat to ward off illness. I plan to introduce memory loss recipes and juice drinks over my website. Eventually if drug companies continue to press regulation, we may be forced to get our vitamins from food unless we get a prescription and pay hiked up prices.

Is Alzheimer's Genetic?

Realize also, not everyone is convinced that Alzheimer's follows a perfect genetic blueprint and that we are doomed if we have the gene (Crook & Adderly, 1998). Research has even shown us people who function well in spite of Alzheimer's diagnoses (Snowdon, Kemper, Mortimer, Greiner, Wekstein, & Markesbery, 1996). Alzheimer's is mainly a synaptic failure, meaning nerves don't connect properly anymore (Selkoe, 2002). If you do believe your symptoms are those of Alzheimer's, be sure to see your physician for early diagnosis imperative in reducing true Alzheimer's.

However, while you still have time to prevent whatever memory loss you do have, change your lifestyle based on what is already known and proven and available to you right now. Let's not line the drug companies' pockets with any more money while we wait for their agenda and place our futures in the balance. Believe me, the prevention available to you now through proper living and eating is far superior to letting your memory fail and taking drugs after the fact. Gaining weight so you can get liposuction makes as much sense as letting memory losses get worse to take drugs!

Other Often Overlooked Forms of Memory Loss

Other than Korsakoff's syndrome caused by heavy alcohol intake and severe amnesia, Alzheimer's wins hands down for causing the worst short-term memory loss problem. Yes, you read me right, alcohol actually can create a worse memory loss problem than Alzheimer's. Head injury and stroke are the most common causes of long-term memory loss. However, before we look closer at serious memory loss problems and their ramifications, let's looking at the many other memory loss problems.

ADHD

First, remember that memory loss is going on in the young as well as the old. Lots of children are having difficulty in school. Many American children eat way too much fast food like French fries filled with dangerous trans fats and lacking the nutrition of whole foods, fruits, and vegetables? The learning disabled and ADHD children and adults suffer poor neurological connections affecting clear thinking and memories and require: Proper rest, nutritious memory vitamins, a diet loaded with real, not processed, foods including a lot of green vegetables like spinach and wheat grass, exercise, lack of stress, and a routine with challenging mental exercise. These would help them; don't drug them unless it's drastic and you've tried all these nutrition methods please. For their future, follow Appendix E lists. Many drugs are for the teachers to look good, and only encourage future drug abuse!

Brain Tumors/HIV

People with brain tumors often have memory loss symptoms and HIV sufferers can as well. Both groups are probably more aware than those with less serious diseases causing memory loss to care for themselves nutritionally with the guidance of their medical doctor. Oncologists and those working with cancer are the most knowledgeable doctors I have met about nutrition and vitamins. Anyone who has been through cancer knows that diet and de-stressing are of utmost importance. As the medical community is increasingly aware of this, so are the drug companies looking for control of vitamins.

The Drug Company Protocol

Drug companies are beginning to realize, there is no one cure for cancer anymore than there will be for memory loss. Tumors don't grow as easily in bodies low in toxins. Neither do other disease forms leading to memory loss. Drug companies know we're figuring this out, and they don't want to give up their expected profits from this elderly epidemic as it grows or give up their position as king of the hill. They have been planning for big profits from Alzheimer's fallout for ages—the day that one big cure arrives. So even though they might know the truth about nutrition, they don't want to share it with us now because it will cost them money.

Though they'd never admit it, they would rather we drag our memories down further every day with junk food, lousy nutrition, and life-styles that will require them to drug away our symptoms. Then, we can thank them for curing us. 'Don't change anything, just wait, we have a cure. You don't have to do a thing.' That's their message, isn't it? They'll do it all. Help is on the way! Haven't they already missed a lot of people we all love? Aren't they missing more everyday? It's too late already, so why wait? They'll be asking you to do everything I'm asking you to do if they ever get control of vitamins!

DON'T FORGET

Fascinatingly enough, following cancer's lead, it appears we in the United States must change our life styles and eat whole unprocessed foods and herbs with cleansing, healing properties if we want to age well. Proper nutrition and vitamins will be the most powerful preventative and healing medicines of the future for all that ails us including memory loss. What we need is accessible and has been provided for us. Let's hope it stays that way/

Thyroid Disorders

Thyroid disorders have always been a quagmire for the mind, mental health, and memory. Those who have hypothyroidism need thyroid replacement hormones in straight order to think properly. Many have been misdiagnosed as mentally ill in the past. Symptoms include: Hair loss, thick nail growth, dizziness, lack of energy, depression, black out spells, cold hands and feet, and poor memory and thinking in general.

Why are these persons' memory losses and other problems so often missed? This time, I lay the reason at the feet of the insurance companies. The rather expensive series of diagnostic tests required to catch hypothyroid disorders are no longer given in full because insurance does not cover them. A cheaper version finds some cases, but misses most.

When symptoms indicate problems with thyroid, practitioners should offer the fuller series of tests and ignore the false negatives. This continues to be a problem in spite of the ongoing symptoms, which often eventually lead to errant diagnoses like bipolar disorder. Then the patients are given incorrect medications and the plot sickens. Some persons seek health store variety thyroid treatments while hoping their doctors will eventually offer them proper prescriptions. However, if any thyroid hormone is ingested from health food stores, the doctors will have even more difficulty diagnosing the problem with their inferior tests covered by insurance. The problem goes round and round, but the result for the person involved is mental weakness, lagging memory, and inability to focus.

You see drug and insurance companies really don't care if we can think well as long as they make money! Please, if you are fortunate enough to begin thyroid hormones after being tested properly with the full thyroid series (about 7 tests), follow the regimen for eating offered in this chapter. One possible reason your thyroid gave out was an overdose of stress and a genetic tendency that cannot handle the poor nutrition and toxins of this life. In many cases, your white blood cells and red blood cells went into a battle to destroy your thyroid. Your system definitely needs high quality nutrition!

Sadly, many elderly and middle-aged people are suffering from deficient thyroid function. People low on thyroid are depressed, tired, bloated, and surely appear demented. Nursing homes are loaded with this memory problem treated as something more serious or not treated at all. Sometimes I think people prefer to keep the elderly tired and worn out so they'll just give up and die in these homes. Doctors in charge of nursing homes could offer more of the amino acid, l-tyrosine, available at health food stores and in wheat grass to those with the symptoms to see if they improve. More elderly people could use l-tyrosine and thyroid assistance in general. Definitely it is an anti-aging hormone deficient in many people who would be in much better health if they could access this basic necessary growth and metabolic hormone when it is lacking.

Epilepsy

Epilepsy is another offender of memory and clear thinking. Due to seizures, which electrically charge these persons' brains, the balance and health of their nervous systems are impeded over the duration of the epilepsy. Often epileptics have received many brain surgeries, implants, and strong medications that produce "drowsiness, sedation, and memory impairments." Damage from epilepsy may impact "memory of facts and events" or "interfere with understanding of language" or the ability to organize thoughts and "cluster information appropriately" (Crook & Adderly, 1989, p. 208).

Due to the fear of seizures, agoraphobia, (the fear of going out), and other anxiety disorders often build. Many with severe epilepsy have panic attacks in fear of having seizures. The panic attack can actually bring on the new seizure. This cycle starts with their experience of an aura, a sensation that can trigger a seizure. The aura becomes a conditioned response whenever one is in a situation that has brought on a seizure in the past. The aura triggers panic, which then insures the seizure. Epilepsy, like so many other illnesses, is a family illness with everyone drawn into seizure prevention. Actually the use of tools available to reduce panic attacks and anxiety disorders could be extremely helpful to epileptics in reducing this vicious cycle. The Midwest Center's program by Lucinda Bassett (2000) would definitely help with the panic attacks and fear of seizures. (Appendix C).

CHAPTER TWO   **JOYCE**

These persons should also do everything they can to insure memory nutritious eating, and possibly go on the ketogenic diet (www.epilepsyfoundation.org). Epileptic person's need proper connection of the nerve synapses from one neuron to the next. This can be affected by nutrition. Wheat grass, phosphatidylserine/PS, PC, choline, lecithin, omega 3 capsules and the other memory supplements plus the ketogenic diet low in carbohydrates and high in fats and greens would place these persons at a big advantage for overcoming seizures and developing a clearer memory. A nutritionist familiar with the diet can guide those with epilepsy toward greater success with their doctor's approval.

Epileptic persons must build lifestyles filled with positive mood building activities such as soothing music, spiritual, physical, and mental exercise. The epilepsy foundation offers local support and career opportunities as well, which are very helpful.

Hormone Imbalance

Finally, hormone imbalances affecting women at menopause create disturbances to normal adult memory. Anyone with symptoms at menopause can tell you. Though we have estrogen products, the safety of the synthetic versions is very controversial. Some doctors are aware and willing to test hormone levels in women receiving estrogen from natural hormonal creams and supplement programs considered to be safe. Wheat grass, DHEA, ginseng, PS, PC, and vitamin E can be helpful to the memory of a person having the hormonal changes of menopause in conjunction with the chosen hormone replacement therapy (HRT) program as tested by an M.D.

DON'T FORGET

Chapter Three

The Keep It Simple—Facts of Serious Memory Loss

Three-Hour Time Line—
Prevent Further Brain Damage with Stroke

An important, often unknown fact about stroke, also called cerebral vascular accident, CVA, or brain attack, is that it requires emergency room attention before three hours passes at a hospital with acute stroke care in order to stop the ongoing brain damage. Thrombolitic medications like altephase, also called tissue plasminogen activators (TPA) are extremely successful in reducing and preventing further brain damage, but only when they are administered within these first three hours. This is a much shorter grace period than the six hours available to reverse heart attacks.

Stroke and Brain Injury Symptoms

On an impact level, if the stroke injury is to the right side of the brain, the limbs can be damaged on the left side. These right-sided lesions often result in drooping facial muscles and slurred speech with the main changes noticeable on the right side of the face. This is the disorder of dysarthria, and does not cause the memory loss of aphasia.

Conversely, when the stroke event occurs to the left side of the brain, the damage to the limbs, if it occurs, will normally occur to the right, and the language use may become affected. Specifically, this disorder on the left side is the aphasia language memory impairment, also affecting some understanding and speaking abilities and the use of language symbols (Reitan & Wolfson, 1992, p. 295). Loss of words due to aphasia can also affect other modes of communication including: naming, spelling, writing, calculating, and reading (Reitan & Wolfson, 1992).

After head injury, similar results can occur. In my experience, the symptoms of amnesia and some aphasia were the most prominent memory losses of head injury (Appendix A).

Alzheimer's, Acetylcholine, and the Hippocampus

Alzheimer's is our largest memory loss problem, but starts differently than other types of memory loss. Initially, Alzheimer's starts out simply enough as the loss of short-term or recent memory caused by the damage started in the hippocampus located deep in the brain. The neurotransmitter fluid, acetylcholine, can no longer travel from neuron to neuron. General forgetfulness and confusion occur first. Later as the plaques and tangles go scurrying about, Alzheimer's spreads and other parts of the brain suffer the damage also. Then, it moves to the long-term memory storage where people's faces, familiar names, and places are stored. Afterwards, these persons do not even recognize their own family members. At that time, problems with the language and vocabulary can also start. Confusion in speaking and inability to express one's self begins to occur. In the beginning, when only short-term memory is impaired, Alzheimer's can respond favorably to medications prescribed by a medical doctor slowing down its fast destructive pace. Whereas, in latter stages of Alzheimer's, though no promises can be made about a cure, it is now advised that even then, the disorder can be alleviated with educationally stimulating activities, routines, and rituals. Diet and physical exercise remain extremely important throughout the disease's cycle. Think of them as nothing less than medical treatment.

Another important point: Impairments can occur individually or simultaneously. Treatment needs may overlap and you may be working to prevent further memory loss maintaining the short-term memory with medication, while also attempting to recover the long-term language memory loss with education.

The medical profession now recognizes what you are learning here: Prevention, and then, early diagnosis are the greatest defense line against Alzheimer's memory breakdown. Aricept, Reminyl and Exelon can stall Alzheimer's at its mid-stage. Cognex, Deprenel, and Hydergine are also very effective. Mementine offers great hope at the late stage, but is still not called a "cure."

What Will Insurance Companies Do Next?

Back in the 70's, speech therapy, physical therapy, and occupational therapy evaluations were routinely ordered by physicians for head injury or strokes, unless the stroke was in the minor category known as a transient ischemic attack (TIA), a sudden episode that can last between a few minutes and 24 hours (Reitan & Wolfson, 1992, p. 197). Beyond this, the physicians requested evaluations during the hospital stay of almost anyone with a stroke or head injury. If the patient received speech therapy in early care, doctors requested follow-up evaluations at home, in the outpatient center, or wherever they went. Therapy continued for long periods whenever therapists recommended it. I worked with many people into their second and third year.

The present insurance climate has changed all that for head injury and stroke. Even Medicare is now a major problem for the memory loss population. Alzheimer's persons were not given any ongoing treatment in the 70's due to the belief that there were no possible improvements. Now that the facts have changed, and science is reporting that indeed the memory loss population does heal, let's see what the insurance companies do next. I can't wait. Remember, all our decisions about people's lives are based on beliefs such as these. When our beliefs and premises are wrong, we set ourselves and other people up for failure.

Realistic Time Lines for Recovery

The period for successful recovery to long-term memory loss affecting language memory has not changed: The first 6 months to a year is truly critical to getting off to the right start, just as resetting a broken arm is crucial to proper healing there. However, don't throw out the idea of retraining the lost memory and language skills beyond that time frame even if you are forced to begin later. You would still attempt to fix a broken arm later on if you had busted it on a safari and could not have it set immediately.

In language memory loss, even when therapy has to wait due to ill health, progress still continues well into the second and third year and beyond. Very often therapists and doctors are not as involved at that time unless paid out of pocket. From my work experience, the stories told here, and case studies of other professionals, mild to significant improvements occur in motivated persons for many years after the stroke's occurrence. An example is the well-known case of actress Patricia Neal, who conquered her loss of language memory over a 6-year period and to the casual observer, became fully recovered. Kirk Douglas and his family have also shown valiant determination in overcoming dysarthria from stroke. In part two, three extraordinary couples with memory loss for words will tell us more about ongoing recovery. Two head injury cases I will share also took six years to recover just as Miss Patricia Neal did. Those with Alzheimer's memory loss experience various time lines dependent upon early detection, which can extend the period of available memory.

Can You Get Them Back After Memory Loss?

Naturally, I have listened to many reports about memory loss journeys. At best, these families and spouses lives always seemed to change significantly. Often the new role-changes for the surrounding family are difficult and sometimes appear almost insurmountable. Elderly spousal caretakers often struggle to research memory loss by themselves overwhelmed by a haphazard, insufficient rehabilitation process. Before a stroke or head injury, which bring on sudden memory loss, the person with language memory loss may have been the healthy spouse. When this is reversed, an already ailing caretaker often becomes unable to keep up with the demanding care and treatment schedule and is caught in a quagmire of confusion even worse than that of the spouse with memory loss. Though there is some warning with Alzheimer's, results are similar. Relationships often change such that the person who has lost memory or language is never exactly the same again. Daddy no longer acts or talks like Daddy once did. Mom is there, but she is not the same as she was. Will Grandma ever be like Grandma again? Can they get them back?

Family Solutions

The families who tell their stories in part two wanted you to know how they coped and adjusted. In general, people I've talked to over the years seem ill-informed at best on this topic, which affects so many people and their loved ones. At the end of the day, the people generally agree, it is less stressful to try to improve someone's memory to communicate than to settle for the alternative; therefore, it's well worth attempting. In the case of stroke and head injury ongoing practice of homework or lost data will generally be rewarded. Relearning and a settling of confusion or disorientation does come in time and with the right attitudes. With Alzheimer's, memory-training does increase functional behavior where there is regular encouragement, consistency, habits, rituals, routine, and cognitive practice. These are ideal actions for enhancing a forgetful confused memory, and therefore, the wisest course of action.

Some Memory Loss Compensation Methods

Even when speaking remains difficult, people with loss of language memory eventually learn other helpful ways of getting by. In life, during therapy, or while doing self-help work, alone or with others, they can compensate by: Foregoing one favorite word for an easier to

DON'T FORGET

remember one, creating a signal to have a spouse pop a word in when they want help, or sometimes, just hearing the sound of the first letter from their companion will do the trick. Some prefer the jump-start of a hand held word-finding device (See Appendices C & D). For those with general and short term memory loss, other compensations help, such as putting up reminder notes in bold spots nearby often forgotten activities, keeping a journal and regularly keeping a schedule on a large wall calendar are very important. Ongoing vocal study of well-known and needed facts also sharpens the mind. Vocal review of home made maps and labeled photos of doctors, friends and family can help as well (Appendices C & D). When one is trying to remember, all kinds of compensations help. Don't forget to have them repeat names of things they are looking for or want to do *out loud* as they go from one room to another either. Hearing things over and over will stimulate recall and prevent forgetting by keeping the mind focused on the objective. And of course, humor is an absolute must for all memory loss! Increased self-sufficiency through improved communication and self-esteem become the strong positive by-product for everyone involved when the wisdom of humor is invoked.

True Family Stories and Dialogues.

To clarify and add to the awareness of memory loss situations, this book contains true stories of other families who lived through stroke and head injury memory loss (part two). The families dialogue at length about typical family and emotional concerns of those with sudden memory loss like their own. There are many important insights they wanted to share with those

CHAPTER THREE   JOYCE

similarly challenged. Their family members lost many abilities in communication, the recall of words, and also in other cognitive areas, such as how to organize their lives effectively and how to reclaim lost pieces of their personhood that faltered with their memory and language problems.

Those learning to cope with the ailment need to hear from others who can share their successes and concerns. So please share your stories with us after you read this so others will know the truth, there is healing after memory loss. People need to hear from many voices armed with solid information. Families often tell heartbreaking stories that would not be so if they had known more about memory loss and the successes of others. Please sign on to www.dontforgetmemoryloss.com and share your stories or testimonials about nutrition. You can also mail them to Don't Forget, P.O. Box 670686, Coral Springs, FL 33006 or just e-mail them to dontforget@bellsouth.net. Please add a sentence in your note indicating that you would permit your letter to be published in the future.

The Foreign Language Metaphor and Unlocking A Door for Memory Loss

Now, we will talk about "traveling" because people who leave home and go to a country of an unknown foreign language know more about memory loss of words, grammar, and language, then they could possibly realize. Understanding the principles of foreign language memory and learning can unlock the door to success for many families and persons with memory loss.

40

Chapter Four

Like the Traveling Language Student

The parallels for learning about memory loss are rich when you consider many things you already experience every day. For example, you may know how it feels to put on a new pair of glasses and be surprised that you were missing so much without realizing it. Normal memory seems to fall away something like that. One day we remember and then suddenly we notice we're forgetting things we never forgot before. Unless we take action to get our daily nutrition of wheat grass or its nutrients, phosphatidylserine, any needed hormones, and keep exercising mentally and physically, slowly our memory could deteriorate. Then one day, we could wake to a more serious situation, more like the people who've had a stroke, head injury, or beginning Alzheimer's. But even then, their dilemma is very similar to something most people have experienced: Visiting a place where the people speak another language.

Being Understood

When visiting a foreign country, it's always pleasant to know something of the language of the inhabitants. Most travelers and students of the language attempt to learn some key phrases and words before walking on foreign soil. Although some surface knowledge of a language can comfort a visitor, the frustrations and challenges of not being understood will be recalled long after the visit is complete. Similarly, after awakening from a head injury or stroke, where injury to

DON'T FORGET

the brain leaves the memory and word loss difficulty, aphasia, the communication dilemma will resemble the experience of the weary, frustrated traveler.

The Hospital Stay Discoveries

The person may first become aware that something is very wrong with their normal method of speaking. Some will be less aware than others. Then, there will be the natural fear and confusion that comes with a shocking discovery that there is a huge difference and inability to remember familiar words well enough to say them. This affects long-term memory storage and is usually overpowered during the hospital stay by other urgent physical problems in: Walking, lifting, feeling, and movement. Meanwhile, the memory loss often waits in the wings for help. Yet, the need and desire to communicate remains strong among humans and does eventually make its way to center stage.

Locked Inside Without A Voice

Actually, the elderly, already less physically capable, who are at the highest risk for strokes, may be more vulnerable without their communication skills than their younger counterpart victims of language memory loss. After a stroke or head injury, in tact communication would help because normal abilities to do things are gone and one must depend upon others. The lack of proper memory for communication to discuss new problems or even ask for help becomes very formidable and frustrating. What's worse is often, those persons with strokes or head injuries are often acutely aware of this

CHAPTER FOUR   JOYCE

dilemma, although the people around them do not perceive this. Let's face it, imagine how scary that must be—to wake up unable to speak, locked inside one's own body without a voice, but perhaps fully aware of the meaning of conversations going on all around you. How is that possible you may ask? It is more than possible; it is typical! Language memory may appear to be totally lost, but in many cases, it is often just very difficult to access. You see, that aceytlcholine can't make the connection to the next neuron when there is an injury. Still memory loss has many different faces! Don't assume all memory loss is the same.

The Confusing Journey Begins!

When patients wake up in this state, unless they're almost comatose or in deep denial, they can begin the confusing journey into this strange new land of lost memory and language feeling very alone and scared— treated as indifferently by the hospital staff as if they were a guest in a foreign country unable to speak the language. Who really takes out time for you when you don't know their language? Very few indeed. Healthy travelers can at least get around, lift things, and manage to help themselves. This, unfortunately, is not true of a person with a stroke or head injury, who may need help with several problems at once in the beginning. As time goes on, the mounting pressures of poor communication become even more upsetting depending upon the person's temperament and responses from people; that is, unless they begin to improve spontaneously, which some do, though many do not.

DON'T FORGET

Confusing Journeys also Happen with Normal Memory

To use the traveling illustration further, back in high school and college, I studied French and enjoyed it tremendously. When I made my first trip to Paris 20 years later, I boned up on my French and had great aspirations of speaking with native Parisians. Although Paris was wonderful, the speed with which the locals responded to my short simple phrases left my head spinning. In spite of a background and interest in French, my understanding was weak. I had not practiced interacting in French for 20 years and my vocabulary was only slightly enhanced by the brief review. By evening, my mind tired of the confusion. My ex-husband and I would return to our quarter's eager to speak English to one another. We would joke, *"It's like they have a different word for everything!"*

Use It Or Lose It

People with loss of memory experience similar moments in their day: Feelings of confusion; of being too slow to keep up in conversations with others; and of needing to use and hear simple, basic phrases. Some of them try and others just give up. This is often related to their disposition and preferences towards speaking in the first place. The highly motivated, gregarious types who love to talk will naturally try harder. This attitude promotes recovery, just as it does in learning a foreign language. *Hearing and talking* assists the speaker in keeping skills sharp and accessible. Success builds on success. Similarly, *use* and *disuse* become key elements in regaining and preserving one's language and speaking

CHAPTER FOUR — JOYCE

skills after memory loss for words is present. Especially when it comes to words, the vocabulary one has forgotten somewhere within, and then fails to use again is easily lost—or as they say, *'use it or lose it.'* In the same way, without practicing a foreign language and building vocabulary and pronunciation, adults learning a foreign language know how hard it is to keep up the skill, much less ever hope to speak fluently. Equally, due to embarrassment or frustration, patients with language memory loss may eventually withdraw and shut out normal verbal intercourse. Sadly, though this may be their own language, they will have less chance of regaining fluency if they give up. By the way, multilingual persons with memory loss for vocabulary words often lose their weaker languages totally.

Some Helpful Activities and Computer Devices for Language and Memory Loss Reconditioning

This is not to say individuals with memory loss should be pushed when they are not well, but it does indicate that they ought to be properly stimulated by activities something like those one might do while learning a foreign language if they have lost language skills.

Some helpful activities include: Hearing and reviewing words aloud with matching labeled pictures or objects from around the house if possible, labeling things in the home, writing and repeating words matched to the pictures for vocabulary practice, and making up sentences about these same words. What kinds of matching words and pictures? All kinds; many are available in books (see Appendix C & D).

DON'T FORGET

If there are also droopy lips and slurred speech, due to motor damage from stroke, muscle exercises are very helpful. This problem alone, however, is not due to language memory loss. However, sometimes one will notice both problems, the slurring muscular loss and also the language memory loss damage at the same time. Daily speaking, singing, writing, or reading aloud is great for both difficulties—slurring and the language memory loss, that is, if the person feels up to it and doesn't mind the idea. Reading out-loud along with an audio book is very stimulating practice for both problems. Just be sure the person can really read again and has their proper spectacles on because vision problems can also intrude with the elderly or after a stroke or head injury.

Software programs are also available and many can be ordered right over the Internet at very reasonable prices through the National Aphasia Association (see www.aphasia.org or Appendix C). My favorite site is www.parrotsoftware.com. Other methods of improvement include the use of a small hand held electronic language device sold at www.gusinc.com for word finding and recall and a personal laptop devoted to language recall called the lingraphica at www.aphasia.com.

Throw away ideas that are overly frustrating or that just don't fit in your family. If you aren't comfortable with computers, then cassette tapes, books, pen and paper will do just fine for relearning and remembering language ideas.

Professional Speech Therapy & Memory Loss Planning

Until you can no longer afford it or insurance drops you, a speech therapist can help you plan properly to be your own. They can inform you of what to look for later when you need help again and reevaluation. They will advise you about what helpful homework activities you can do on your own at home: What is enough? What's too much? When is a good time? How do you approach these ideas with the memory loss person in mind? They may even allow you to watch them work with your family member so you can imitate and create helpful homework together. Plan. Plan. Plan. Review and study is going to be needed for a while, even after therapists are gone. Make the most of the time while they are there.

Medicare

What if after the therapist leaves, the person with memory loss seems to be unable to learn anymore? You may want to wait a week or more before asking them to do any homework. *But please, don't stop working on the memory loss after you lose your speech professional because of Medicare problems or insurance limits or some announcement that no more improvements can be made.* Medicare reductions and limits of $1500 per patient are ridiculous and insulting when three to four different types of therapists must share that amount. Plus, the therapists and doctors are people and eventually may be forced to give up or go away. The medical circumstances and reasons are not always in their control. Hopefully, they will be available at reasonable rates to consult your home memory-training and language work.

Variety is the Spice of Life

Naturally, no one wants to do homework alone all

the time. Yet, in many cases, a friend may be a better helper than a spouse. In other cases, a grandchild may be very happy to do word games, and perhaps the activity would be fun for them because of a special relationship between an elderly person and the young person. In other cases, a daughter or son, who worked well in the past with the person having the memory loss, may be able to do what a spouse cannot do. Some spouses, like the ones in part two of this book, were able to be extremely helpful in the actual study process. All were helpful encouragers. So how could some couples work together on memory and language? Perhaps they always did projects well together and that is one of the reasons they got married. Others I have known and seen in the past could not work well together. Many therapists don't even want spouses to try because they fear it may be upsetting. I believe there are all kinds of people and couples. I happen to know some people manage to work together even on this problem rather nicely once the attitudes are expectant, accepting, and positive. And, it never hurts to try.

Assisting Without Working Side by Side

Don't be upset if working together doesn't work out. Follow the other routes because there are so many! And remember, all help is not direct help. Putting some homework together, encouraging and reviewing it may be necessary, but does not constitute working together side by side, which is much more tedious and may be the reason agitation occurs.

Some persons who understand computers may just want to work alone with their computer if it is up and running and someone can lead them to the websites, e-

CHAPTER FOUR   **JOYCE**

mail, and support group sites. Others may need to be given some instruction to start using the computer. So a spouse may want to set up a computer and learn a bit from the speech therapist. Some therapists do not know computers, so the websites and software are mentioned above and in Appendix C. The idea is get some helpful appropriate activities going.

Also attendance at adult day programs with word games and activities to sharpen thinking skills can often prove to be acceptable and are often routinely available. Check them out first for fit if you are unsure about attending. Call your speech therapist consultant to ask her opinion after reviewing the group. Finally, your own family may wish to spice up this homework by using many of the different methods and people to help and provide variety.

Slow Down, Pause and Wait for Eye Contact

There are some helpful keys that will assist your family during this period of life. During the first year after a stroke or head injury or when you notice language is difficult for an Alzheimer's person, use a slower pace in speaking to the person with memory loss and look at them when you speak to them. Also, be sure they are looking at you! Use more pauses and fewer words, if possible, if you are known to be a fast talker. Don't be condescending or treat them like a child, but do avoid excess wordiness. You are dealing with a healing brain or weakened one. The person with language memory loss will give slow and sometimes even delayed responses as they take needed time to think about what they are saying. This can be expected as they learn to reconnect the words into sentences again. This slow delivery may speed up a bit over time with an encouraging attitude if the person spoke rapidly before, but not in all cases, especially where there are the following: Severe perseveration (repetition), apraxia (inability to speak at will), or heavy use of jargon, (long incomprehensible strings of utterance). See Appendix A.

Plateaus Happen—Be Patient— Forward Acceleration Will Return

Again, envision yourself speaking in a less known language, and then, think of the person with memory loss for words as having the same experiences. In my own foreign travels, it was when I was slowly pulled into short friendly conversations while shopping and walking about that I was able to feel my way and monitor how I was doing. I was able to think and register the new vocabulary, phrases and pronunciation. This happens to the person with memory loss, too. Take your time in speaking, and trust me, if they are respected for not giving up during this period of speaking challenges, they will naturally do the best they can to process and respond to everything going on. Don't let them fool you. Frustrated as they may be, no one wants to lose their main method of social communication. *If the environment is accepting and loving and they are healthy enough, they will attempt to improve and can learn again.* Sometimes learning will accelerate; other times it will appear to plateau. Don't give in to impulses to shut them out or to constantly communicate for them; out of pain and frustration, they might be tempted to give up, but you will only stall their progress this way.

CHAPTER FOUR   J O Y C E

No Pressure in Public, Please, and Think Before Talking For Them

Consider this. In Paris, when I was rushed to answer people quickly as a foreigner, I couldn't catch my breath and think about the last thing I'd learned because of the new moment's pressure. Often I just felt flustered even if I had some ideas about the word or what I wanted to express. In talking to persons with memory loss for words, develop a comfortable rhythm. There is no need to jump in when they are trying to speak unless you can see that they want you to. You will know by the clear message on their face or by some other signal the two of you have devised together whether or not your input would feel helpful or hurtful. A tap of the index finger to the nose might work beautifully when the person is capable of such an idea. When you see him or her grabbing at the air obviously asking you 'please' for 'the word.' That is an okay time to give it. Don't frustrate the person at those moments. Other times, you will not jump right in when it looks just as hard, if he or she has expressed not wanting your help while attempting to meet the learning challenge. At some point, you will learn, even when the person said they don't want help, you might give it now and then to help avoid embarrassment.

Prompting the First Sound

Often prompting the first sound or letter might be all the person needs to hear from you to recall the word. Remember, when the person is relaxed and can review his or her thoughts with a little more time to think, understanding of what is said and ability to remember old words will greatly increase. This is true for memory loss of stroke, head trauma, and mild Alzheimer's persons, both young and old. When the person feels he or she can handle a party or social environment, don't hold them back because of this preference for a relaxed environment—go! They may only want to do something like this occasionally and we only go around once! Follow these simple guidelines, prompt them occasionally and encourage them on during the outing. Afterwards, applaud them for their bravery. Be grateful to be in your own shoes instead of theirs. They may even become more mellow and easy to be with at these times than before.

Comparing Normal Language Memory and its Development to Memory Loss Developments

Over the first year after language memory loss occurs, it is helpful to realize how language naturally develops in both children and foreign language students. Consider how a one-year old communicates during the first year of life. Babies listen for a long time before they jump in and begin to talk with meaning. Not until toddlerhood a few years later do some real language skills set in. *The extent of mastery children develop depends upon what they heard before they began to talk.*

A Refresher Course

Give the same kind of timeline and expectations to one recalling words and relearning to speak. Stroke and head injured with memory loss have an open door to learning that is keen and will expand their language base rapidly until hitting those learning plateaus. However, if in the beginning, they sit back and do nothing for their memory loss, they will be much less likely to rekindle their language to the best levels. But remember, they are not children. They have heard these words before. *They are students needing a refresher course.* They are thinking adults presently short on vocabulary memory and other language skills. Let words and sentences settle in on them as they heal.

Talking and Adjusting Together at Home

During your days together, comment aloud to them peacefully about the activities of daily life: What they are doing, what you are doing. A natural response to such an activity might be that they will slowly begin to reflect verbally also. Even if they do not respond, keep it up so they overhear normal vocabulary regularly and not just from a television set. There is no innate desire within human beings to respond to a piece of equipment. There is a desire for human interaction. Give them time to adjust as they talk to you and learn daily, steadily, progressively. As far as their language work, each day should include intense homework review or study for only a half hour to an hour if they are able and want to participate or sit up to a computer and work.

Computers

Though unfamiliar territory for some, the computer may be a lot more help than many people would realize beyond practicing vocabulary. One can diary, journal, produce letters and send e-mails much more efficiently using a keyboard than by hand writing with the left hand if the right is impaired. Making lists, writing things down, and keeping organized are priorities these persons will need to develop and be responsible about—to the best of their ability and of course memory loss will affect this, yet the practice will help them remember. Scheduling and staying in touch are things language memory loss persons can learn to do again because of the computer. Actually, being able to write and communicate through writing is very motivating and empowering for the memory loss person, who must eventually become the primary one involved in the recovery process.

Nix Negativity

If I could not have gone home from the Paris trip after a few weeks, believe me, I would have been quite focused on my language and memory problems until I caught up! I would have worked a computer rather than face the French all day. Although there were English-speaking people in Paris, I desired to interact in French. People with loss of word memory due to this condition of aphasia also want to get back to talking the natural way, without thinking about it so much, but they very often cannot do so right away. They are as impatient to return to normal as you are, but need to believe that improvement is possible. For that reason, any negativity regarding memory-training must go! Pass by the nay-sayers! Pull out the Internet and e-mail!

CHAPTER FOUR **JOYCE**

Vital! Memory Loss Support Groups & E-Mail

Memory loss persons very much need the camaraderie of memory loss support groups, aphasia for head injury or stroke, or separate Alzheimer's, stroke, and head injury groups, but at the same time they are initially conflicted about this and can have trouble in the support groups. Imagine being frustrated in a support group because you cannot communicate with each other! Nevertheless, if a friend or spouse goes along to an aphasia memory loss, stroke, head injury, or Alzheimer's support group, they will feel they are being represented and eventually find creative ways to compensate and communicate. At least, by listening, they will realize they are not alone and so will you. Plus, you will both learn coping skills from others who have been on this journey. So do go along with them. Zero in on that group that exemplifies your greatest needs. The memory loss person could fit into more than one group at a time: a computer group, e-mail group, Internet support group, a young stroke group, or a cognitive therapy group. All these are discussed on www.innovativespeech.com.html and through the NAA at www.aphasia.org. Some people even find additional low priced private therapy through the groups using university therapists in training. Groups are often held at university speech clinics and at the local hospital. When you have to live with this memory loss impairment day in and day out, the encouragement and stories of others will cheer all of you on and are extremely important! Information and understanding brings about the positive, expectant attitude (Appendix C).

DON'T FORGET

The Hard Lessons—Normal Memory or Relearned—Require Patience and Humor

For one who has a severe language memory loss problem, speaking may always be somewhat daunting for the rest of that person's life. Still, such speakers do improve, and will gradually attempt more difficult conversational tasks. When my foreign conversations moved away from simple things like asking directions or other easy to recall greetings, I found that my vocabulary skills were still too weak to pick up on idioms or to carry on lengthy, in-depth conversation. This is also the final, difficult milestone for the person with memory loss for words.Once again, if a lengthy in-depth conversation is necessary, be patient.

During my foreign trips, it was a daunting task to explain anything in French like what I am presently writing in English. Explanations, descriptions and details are also a real challenge after language memory loss. As performance improves, there will be breakthroughs to moments of greater clarity, confidence and ease in speaking. Yet there may be left over difficulties in more abstract concepts and reasoning. Except in passive mediums like television, typical conversation requires many subtle explanations, detailed descriptions, and the constant juggling of slang and idioms. We usually interpret these culturally, in the tempo of our day-to-day social life—this is where it gets tough having memory loss of language; whether one has it seriously or lightly. Memory and language successes are strongly affected by the person's own temperament, the family or caretaker's understanding and, believe it or not, everyone's sense of humor.

CHAPTER FOUR **JOYCE**

Expectant Attitude Point I: Veil of Disability or Challenge and Love of Learning

It's a well-known fact that immersion in a country with a foreign language one wishes to learn assists language memory and learning. In the same respect, back and forth conversation strongly helps language memory loss. Unfortunately, after stroke or head injury, a person with language memory loss differs from a language student in one huge way—the student's learning situation is by choice and not forced upon him or her. However, the person afflicted by loss of language memory lives with the heavy veil of a *disability* hanging over him or her. This sense of being *disabled* prevents the person and family from embracing the new *learning challenge* fully and is especially difficult to accept in social situations. However, those learning a foreign language, feel differently since they are proud of their challenge, but are also just as uncomfortable in social situations where they can't remember the words or 'how to say it.'

At earlier points in one's life, prior to memory loss, when one feels weak in an area, one takes a class, finds out what to do, and basically learns more about the situation. After stroke or head injury, these persons are often left feeling bereft of previous abilities and options to learn. However, as for their options to learn, they are still quite possible! However, without a hopeful attitude, they become puzzled and bewildered by their memory loss and about how to fit in. Unless a comfortable level of patient expectation and acceptance of the necessary learning and studies ahead is reached by everybody, including themselves, their feelings of inadequacy may persist for a long time on many levels. If they give up or refuse to try, their problems may also remain disappointing.

When their friends stop being friendly, that also hurts. Be positive and hopeful with them, enlisting them to become study partners instead! And when the memory loss person doesn't want to work, let them stew. They'll come around again. Just keep making the offer to study or review recommended homework material. Bring the right friend around to help and they may pull the homework out themselves!

The Expectant Attitude Point II:
To Journey is Better than to Arrive

If I could overstress one point in this book, this is it! How many times we struggle throughout life and fail to realize that pain creates new growth and is necessary and helpful. Not that anyone wishes pain or should cause pain to another. But once it is here, what can we do? We think we should be able to simply stop, sit back on our laurels and rest or retire after a certain point. We learn as we live that life isn't really like that. More and more, in a world like our own, people of every age know: One can never stop growing and learning. When there is a difficulty or learning challenge, like memory loss, we are only being asked to do what we should already be doing anyway, continuing to grow. This is true for the person with the memory loss and for loved ones and friends. When we stop growing, we die.

For evidence, look to Viktor Frankl's book, <u>Man's Search for Meaning</u> written about his concentration camp survival. Frankl explains it was only after prisoners gave up hope that they failed to thrive and began to die. Those who survived did not even realize they were free at first

CHAPTER FOUR — JOYCE

even when liberation arrived, much as our memory loss friends give up before the memory loss battle is lost, while freedom could be just around the bend if they did their homework! The most intriguing point Frankl makes is that the end result was only a small part of the prisoners' struggle. The larger challenge was to respond responsibly and with dignity no matter what came. Having an even higher purpose like aiming for freedom to help someone else or preventing this fate for others gave life even more meaning whether freedom was ever attained or not. Some prisoners who lived hurt others to do so and lost at finding meaning during the process, while others continued to behave responsibly regardless. People needed a purpose and were more alive during the process of attaining the goal than they were after they achieved it.

Likewise, the end result is not the only reason to try to improve after memory loss because while living through the process simply expecting recovery, one may never even notice the challenge has been met until it has passed by. The expectant attitude is one of proactive involvement, superior to a hopeful attitude, which is simply passive and won't get the job done. The process of growing itself becomes the norm of life again and is the most valuable part—returning the meaning and purpose to life.

The journey, as they say, is better than the arrival. In the case of an expectant attitude for memory recovery this must be understood. For the journey to be successful, one must cease to think of the seeming impossibilities of a *disability* and be a *student* of whatever life hands us realizing that being responsible and doing the right and dignified thing at every moment is how the opportunities, possibilities and healings are reopened to us, or so Frankl expresses. I can relate! I proactively expect you can relate also because hoping just isn't enough to cut the mustard!

How to Come Home

In a sense, the memory loss survivors with language loss are something like visitors in their own culture, struggling to find themselves and remember words well enough to communicate effectively. Although they usually continue to learn and find the words locked inside, they are not simply able to jump on an airplane and come home in one day as I was. Memory loss recovery can be a lengthy process that varies for different people. Well-known language memory loss aphasia specialist, Hildred Schuell (1974, p. 87) notes that a person with the language memory loss can be compared to "someone trying to use a language that he once knew but now recalls only imperfectly." If language memory loss individuals are home, hopefully they won't feel like strangers in their own home. Allow them to feel that their plight is acceptable, as you would want for yourself if you were in their shoes. This is hard for everyone at first.

Demographics

Remember, one day you too may have your own memory related difficulties. Stroke is the third greatest health risk in America and second greatest cause of disabilities with one third of its numbers affected by language memory loss. Alzheimer's is described as a disease of catastrophic proportions by the U.S. Department of Health and Human Services. With 4 million suffering from it, 11 million are expected in the ranks by 2005. Head injury claims 5.3 million with disabilities. The other forms of memory loss are also formidable. Age-associated memory impairments (AAMI) are everyday conversation topics with 'senior moments' referred to regularly. Memory loss is just no respecter of persons. The public is generally unaware of the phenomenal proportions of this problem for all of us—at present and in the future!

A Family Problem: Listen in as One Spouse Expresses Her Serious Frustration

Naturally, the frustration levels after life with memory loss can become very apparent and obviously exasperating. As one spouse commented to me of her husband, "It would be better [for him] to lose an arm or a leg than to lose the ability to speak!" (Spouse of an aphasic patient, personal communication, 1995). Thus the language memory loss that is initially only an irritation overshadowed by threatened life and limb becomes the most important issue as time marches on and the loss of communication and being locked inside oneself becomes the focal problem.

Can You Relate?

Perhaps each person can recall a time when you were frustrated in a language situation, either being in a different culture, around unusual terms, dialects, or being overwhelmed in a public speaking situation. Ever get the wind knocked out of you? Possibly you might even know of someone in a medical situation where they lay prone in

DON'T FORGET

a hospital bed with a throat ventilator, which is becoming increasingly common and an almost automatic procedure in many elderly, surgical, and accident patients. However, the ventilator inhibits them from communicating with those around them. In this day and age, it is very possible to be kept from speaking a last word just as one comes to the end of life and desperately wants to say a few important things before breathing that final breath.

Imagine You on that Bed!

For a moment, imagine this is you in a hospital bed with language memory loss or other problems holding you back from speaking aloud yourself, but still in your case, you are aware and awake with fine short-term memory. Perhaps you understand everything going on around you, but those around you do not know this and begin to raise their voices in speaking to you, thinking you will understand them better that way. What if you know exactly what you want to say to them, but are unable to verbalize the right words for several days or weeks? You could write, but you do not realize it, and you would need some help to get started anyway. The persons who visit you don't know you have any thoughts about what to say. Also you are just plain weak and can't ask for a pen if you do think of it, and no one else knows or thinks to offer you one, much less to assist you or offer a writing platform or other things you may need, but can't ask for.

A Student's Surgery—A Moment of Gratitude

A student of mine experienced a moment similar

to memory loss after surgery and put it this way in an assignment: "I wanted to ask for food but I had absolutely no control over my oral muscles enabling me to talk. I was fearful although I knew the capacity to talk was due to the effect of the anesthesia still present in my body. I felt so relieved when I could finally communicate my desires. At that moment, I knew I needed to be able to talk because I was extremely hungry. I doubt that it was more than a few minutes between my awakening and my first word, but it felt as if my language ability was gone for months or even years. The insignificant time I spent wishing I could talk touched me tremendously. I thought about the number of patients with anomia [a type of aphasia memory loss] resulting from strokes, including my grandmother who suffered from aphasia months before her death."

Memory Loss Assumptions with Ventilator Problems— Damaging Untrue Remarks

That's also very similar to what you might go through if you had a throat ventilator for oxygen after stroke, head injury, or surgery. Language memory loss or no memory loss at all, you wouldn't be able to ask for the inexpensive little plastic speaking valve or speaking ventilator. You could not talk at all without this technology, but most people don't even know to ask for them and are unable to unless someone else steps forward (Iskowitz, 1998b). Guess what? If it were you, you would still be you inside that body unable to speak. Even if you had a stroke, there would not normally be short-term memory loss of the ongoing moment-by-moment events.

DON'T FORGET

Don't Let Last Words Be Lost Words

Every day, the common needs of those who cannot speak because of memory loss or other causes are missed. These problems are commonly assisted by speech therapists who, unfortunately, are not always on managed care plans anymore for every problem that comes up. So only alert family members may be able to call the doctor, or request the restored speaking ability by ordering a speaking valve or ventilator. And please, if ever you experience this with a loved one, don't let an untrained observer, possibly even from the nursing staff tell you, 'the person had a stroke and can't talk anyway so they don't need the speaking ventilator.' How damaging if such a comment is made in the patient's presence and how important to give a person in critical condition a chance to try to speak. No one knows whether the person can speak or recall language, not even the one with memory loss, not until they try to speak and have a proper speaking apparatus for doing so. Now you know, in ventilator cases, only you may have the power to make sure your family member's *last words won't be lost words.*

Comprehension is Often in Tact

Even with the inability to remember or speak after stroke or head injury, comprehension may be good. The recovery of comprehension will return before the speaking and may be only mildly reduced in many memory impairments. Realize that those with memory loss may understand every word you speak, just like you could possibly understand a foreign language before you

CHAPTER FOUR   JOYCE

could speak it. So watch what you or others say in front of them. Be very careful not to put them in the grave or elsewhere with your words. If you have it in you, please be encouraging during bedside visitations and enlist others to do the same, including the medical professionals! The giving up that can occur needlessly at those moments is heartbreaking.

Part Two

Chapter 5

True Family Stories with Insurance Affects

Chapter 6: 1-11

The Families Speak to You
Eleven Concerns after Serious Memory Loss

Chapter 7

Amazing Memory Loss Stories
—To Do and Not To Do

DON'T FORGET

Chapter Five

True Family Stories with Insurance Affects

The four families spoke to me candidly and everyone in the book asked me at some point to use their real names, which I declined to do. In this group, each had one family member with a stroke causing memory loss, which also affected language memory. The person with memory loss is listed first, followed by the family member most involved in their healing. We will call them: Bob and Kay, Clay and Pam, Sarah and Eve, and Steve and Laura. Except for Sarah and Eve, a mother and daughter dyad, the other three are couples.

Overlapping Losses

The four persons had many overlapping losses and symptoms to speak about. Often there was more than one memory loss difficulty. If you review the glossary in Appendix A for more detailed definitions, you will see the list of possibilities. An example would be that disorders of dysarthria (poor pronunciation, not a memory problem), aggrammatism (poor grammar), jargon (nonsense words), and say, dyslexia (reading difficulty) could occur simultaneously. Thus, I use terms like "lost language memory." While I'd like to be descriptive, it's important to simplify. Redefining the fine nuances can turn into a distraction sometimes. Confusion has plagued this disorder in the past, so please review these definitions as needed, but do not let them overwhelm you. Remember to 'keep it simple stupid' (KISS), an important dynamic.

CHAPTER FIVE   JOYCE

Who Spoke During Interviews

In all but one case, the caregivers told the family story. You see Bob and Clay had passed away after their recoveries. Their wives spoke to me after their deaths. Sarah was unable to speak at the time of the interview because her stroke was recent and her memory and language disorder were severe. Steve did a great job of telling his own story along with his wife, who was no longer a caregiver for him at the time of our interview.

Each caregiver had that role for varying lengths of time with different degrees of caretaking incumbent upon them. This role shifted with the severity of the stroke and the levels of recovery. Only in the case of Steve and Laura, could both share their long-term experiences, which are invaluable.

Clay's Recovery

Sarah, Clay, and Steve all had complete losses in language memory and usage called global aphasia. This term implies complete loss of ability in memory and using words correctly. Many such global aphasic patients look almost vegetative after the stroke at the hospital. Clay did not, according to his wife, and had absolutely no other problems from his stroke, not even a weak arm or leg, only the global language memory loss. Apparently, Clay had some comprehension evident by his clear grasp of the dilemma and his capacity for researching and recovering from the loss of language memory. His serious personal struggle was entirely about his inability to communicate and his concerns for his wife and family and that his life was at very high risk. Clay was also the youngest, 44, of

DON'T FORGET

the stroke persons interviewed. Three years before his death, he did manage to recover almost completely from this total language memory problem. In fact, he directed much of his own therapy.

Neurological Repair

However, it is not unusual that Clay or Steve recovered almost completely. Serious memory loss for language can and does heal with rehabilitation. Sometimes a recovery happens almost suddenly at the beginning. More often, the healing from this memory loss occurs in connection with frequent therapy, perseverance, and regular outside stimulation. The initial symptoms make the memory loss of global aphasia the most feared and devastating type of language memory loss. Most people do not expect the person to ever speak intelligibly again or realize that the person still possesses any mental capacity. However, that just is not true. I have seen many such persons come out of their dilemmas time and time again. Their cases resemble the state of a computer hard drive without a monitor. The lights may be off, but somebody is home. Locked inside the brain, the information can be accessed as new pathways and connections develop and healing takes place. In neurological repair, neural pathways do find new ways to connect. The neurotransmitter fluid, acetylcholine, travels when stimulation to one area of nerves affects and reconnects them. New 'synapses' occur. Touch to one sensitive nerve will cause others to come alive as well. Next thing you know changes happen in associated areas. Lost language centers are accessed in this way.

CHAPTER FIVE   **JOYCE**

Stimulation for one word produces others. And now, science is beginning to report that damaged brain cells are healing.

Stem Cell Research

Reports of studies attesting to recoveries have always been available to therapists. So in the past, no one but the therapists in the trenches knew that recoveries have been going on all along especially when there was good insurance coverage with some time to work on the problem. Christopher Reeve is one known example of someone whose improvements after spinal cord injury are changing health care and showing that nerve cells actually do heal. He did not achieve his healing overnight or by sitting back and waiting for it. In his case and for many others, adult stem cell research could hold much promise.

Insurance Problems without Recovery Guarantees

After managed care came, without guarantees of recovery, previously good insurance plans began to disappear or offered scant coverage with stipulations and barriers making treatments almost impossible for therapists to secure. The consequences were devastating. With few insurance funds covering therapy properly, doctors were left scratching their heads and pausing to wonder, just what was absolutely urgent based on funds? Exactly how to make proper decisions about ongoing therapy recommendations had been up to therapists in the past. Families were left with no say in the situation at all.

DON'T FORGET

Doctor and Therapist Reports

For economic reasons, many well-meaning doctors in this day and age often report to families with a member who had a memory loss affecting language that they will probably never speak again. Why? Mainly because the funds are not there to adequately rehabilitate the patient anyway. As a result, doctors unwittingly come to believe these disorders must be close to impossible to eradicate, though that has never been true. Even the best insurance plans often unreasonably expect an extremely good response in a few days or weeks of therapy or funds are simply cut. Many cases come around, but not usually so immediately. Each case is unique to the individual.

All a therapist has to do to lose services is report a day or two of poor responses and the insurance for speech therapy may be terminated. No one argues the point anymore. The battle is so difficult. Many of the younger doctors are unaware of the many recovery successes that occurred back when treatment went on for a few months or even a year or more. In fact, non-professional treatment and healing can and should go on indefinitely long past the second year. Families need to be prepared early on about ways this can be done. In three of the families reporting here, work continued past the second year with positive results from all who continued to press on. Neurological speech, language, and memory impairments require persistent treatment and often start out as a total loss of memory and communication skills.

CHAPTER FIVE **JOYCE**

Family Conversations

As you are learning, lost language memory disorders are multi-faceted. To keep the focus on the memory loss aspect of the stroke, I limited the conversation with these families to that issue as much as possible. This task was often difficult because this was not the only issue. For Sarah, the recent case who could not speak at the time of my visit, her lost self-help skills for daily living activities were initially the most crucial issues to her daughter, Eve, who added that the lost communication severely impeded the act of care giving. Sarah suffered such a complete loss that Eve had much to say about the impact of her mother's memory problem. The longest of the cases, Steve, and his wife, Laura, were a couple who had lived with the husband's lost language memory for 14 years, and had become so extremely knowledgeable about stroke and memory loss that it was sometimes difficult for them to sort out "stroke" health problems from "aphasia" the memory loss problem. Their insights are surprising and shocking. Read them closely because they know what is typical. Bob and Clay were also long-term cases and their wives agreed that loss of language memory eventually became their main problem or the showstopper, you might say, of their stroke problems. Initial talk about the stroke and ill health receded, and eventually talk about the memory loss and communication took over.

Meet the Families Who Spoke

The family members themselves included people from many age ranges. Pam and Clay had young children

DON'T FORGET

and adolescents, who all remained in the home. Eve, Sarah's daughter, and Bob and Kay had teenaged and grown children. Bob's children were older stepchildren to Kay, who married Bob while the children were living with their mother. Eve had the most generations to deal with in her life. As the grown female child and caregiver of her elderly mother, this adult caregiver was also raising her own teenaged children and helped care for grandchildren born to one of her grown children. Lots of difficult situations crept up on all three of these families involving discipline and future living arrangements. Laura and Steve, on the other hand, had only grown children already out of the house.

In viewing the age range differences among the persons with memory loss, Clay was 44 and the youngest of the four at the point of his stroke onset. Bob was 60. Sarah was 78. Steve, who had survived the longest, was 68 at the time of the interview, but was 54 when his stroke first occurred. These cases showed the wide range of possible variations within the disorder. As might be expected after stroke, individual health varied widely. While the caretakers were generally in good physical health in this study, that is often not the case in other families who are less fortunate than these. These persons all came from a variety of economic and career backgrounds.

Education Levels

Educational levels were fairly homogeneous with some college education and degrees held by all but adult caregiver, Eve, and her mother, Sarah, and who

CHAPTER FIVE — JOYCE

experienced the most emotional distress in that role. The memory losses ranged from Bob's mild to moderate one to the other three more severe types. Sarah's case was both acute (meaning it was in the early stage) and severe, but was subject to changes as it moved toward a more chronic, longer state. That is why it is important to present it here though her long-term success or failure is not known at this time. People need to realize the beginning can be tough if there is no help. Other long-term cases had time to gain some understanding and reviewed their thoughts in retrospect while living with the disorder for a time. Eve, on the other hand, was going through a fire created by a lack of help. In the end, it is apparent this problem was related to the maneuverings of the insurance industry.

Dying

In the two cases that died, reflections about their deaths became part of the interview conversation. Obviously, health has been compromised after a stroke and longevity may be diminished. Remember that though Bob and Clay eventually died, both of those men went through rehabilitation and enjoyed their final years more because they improved their memory and ability to communicate again as a result. Others who survive to enjoy their recovery, like Steve, are fortunate. Not all get the necessary help to recover, like Sarah, Eve's mother. This is unfortunate, as it would increase the likelihood of a successful survival. The point is that those who are dealt the misfortune of becoming less vital due to stroke should attempt to get well and regain memory skills necessary for ongoing mental, social, and physical well being. Steve outlived his stroke and memory loss for 14 years, rehabilitated himself and others over the years, and from all reports, he is still going strong! The truth is the person may survive and become healthy again, like Steve did, and what then if the memory loss is not dealt with?

Spiritual Coping

Essentially, the families interviewed represented a wide cross-section of cultural and religious types. From their own reports, religious views and spirituality were helpful and supportive to some participants and assisted them in coping with the severity of their concerns. In addition, all of the families mourned over the losses from their family members' pre-stroke states in a variety of ways. Those losses of their ability to recall and use language usually were also complicated by characteristic physical anomalies that often accompany stroke, such as disabilities in walking or using one's hands or arms. Three of the four individuals with stroke in my study had also dealt with these other physical losses and grieved them simultaneously to the memory loss.

Agreement without Hesitation about Memory Loss

Each family reported, without hesitation, that without the loss of language memory the other losses would have been bearable. The families each agreed that if a person loses their ability to walk or work with their hands and then also loses the ability to maintain intelligent communication, the loss in the last area would probably determine their fate more than the loss of hand usage and mobility. Inability to remember for communication's sake would be the disabling process that would separate and isolate the person socially and then go on to isolate them physically as well in the future.

Individual Family Profiles

Family One: Bob and Kay

The first interview was held with a widowed schoolteacher, Kay. She was Bob's third wife and had been married to Bob for eight years prior to his stroke. It was her first marriage and his third one. At the time of his stroke, Bob was 60 and Kay was 39. Bob had eight children, four children from a first marriage, who were grown, and four teenagers from a second marriage, who lived with Bob and Kay.

The family's life revolved around Bob and his well-known radio personality and voice, which set the context for their social and cultural relationships in a Christian community. For their first two years of marriage, they lived alone as a couple, both working in careers centered at their church where they had met one another. He was manager of the Christian radio station there. She was a schoolteacher at the school on the same premises. Initially, they took the four younger children, the ones from the second marriage, for visitations. After a time, the four children moved in with Bob and Kay and were all living with them for several years when their father had two strokes one occurring within a few days of the other. The oldest daughter was home at the time after two years away at college. The second daughter was in her freshman year of college out of state. The two younger children were in high school.

In his radio career, Bob had worked with many famed personalities, including Lorne Greene, Rich Little and Gene Autry. At one time, he was Loretta Lynn's boss. Helen Hayes knew of his Christian reading work and remarked of him, "He had the definitive voice to read the Bible." Then six years before his death by heart attack at age 66, he suffered the two strokes that would disrupt his unique gift for communication. Despite the difficulties the language memory loss disorder caused for him, he continued to work as the radio manager until his death, compensating for his lost language skills by using old recordings of his own voice in the radio studio.

Meanwhile Kay, the stepparent, was pressured into taking on the new roles of disciplinarian, caretaker, and occasional speech therapist after the stroke occurred. If Bob had not been in the radio career, his language disorder would most likely have been classified as mild to moderate. Under the circumstances, however, the intensity of the language memory loss problem was serious for Bob because of his career in media using his speech, language, and voice daily to provide for his family and as his life's work.

Family Two: Pam and Clay

The second interview was held with another widow, Pam, whose husband Clay died in 1992, five years post stroke, from a ruptured aneurysm. An autopsy revealed that Clay strained himself and ruptured his aorta in 1987 and concluded that this activity brought on the

CHAPTER FIVE — JOYCE

cerebral vascular accident. Clay was only 44 years old when this stroke occurred, while Pam was 37. This couple had been married only 7 years before Clay incurred the stroke, which resulted in complete language memory loss called "global aphasia." Pam was Clay's first wife and the couple had three daughters. At the time of the stroke, their oldest daughter, Renee, was 13 years old. Clay had adopted her when she was six years old. The younger two daughters were four and five.

Clay had been the CEO and owner of a furniture company. The family had moved out of state and expanded their business from three to seven stores. Owning the business was his life long dream. His wife assisted him in this endeavor on occasion as treasurer, but mainly ran the household. Naturally, such a career involved the use of speaking and memory skills for selling and also reading, writing, and computation skills for the understanding of the accounting of their business endeavors. With a language memory disorder of such a severe variety as global aphasia, Clay had lost nearly all such memory for language abilities. With very little outside encouragement, according to his wife, his dilemma and pursuit for improvement of his language memory was very serious and confounding. In spite of this, Clay was very persevering in his pursuit of rehabilitation, so much so that eventually he became President of the National Aphasia Association (NAA). Pam continued to run the association for some time after Clay's death.

DON'T FORGET

Family Three: Sarah and Eve

The third participant interviewed was Eve, aged 49, a daughter turned into her mother's caregiver, who moved her stricken mother, Sarah, into her nuclear family's home with her husband and two teenaged children in the home. A third child, a daughter, lived outside of the house raising her own children. Eve described her struggle to work out her life with her children while attempting to care for her mother. Of the four cases, Eve was experiencing the deepest difficulties at the acute stage of aphasia and stroke at the time of our interview. In fact, she was in severe crisis and believed she had suffered a mental breakdown over the stress of her situation just prior to the interview.

Her mother, Sarah, was 78 and had the stroke and complete language memory loss of global aphasia six months prior to our conversation. Her language abilities on the day of my visit included crying, moaning, groaning, the use of jargon, and occasional outbursts of "No, no, no, no, no." Before the stroke event, her mother lived in her own condominium and was functioning independently.

Family Four: Steve and Laura

Steve, and his wife and former caregiver, Laura, were the only couple who dialogued together with me in their interview at one time. Steve had suffered a stroke and complete memory loss of global aphasia in 1985, 14 years prior to the interview. His was the most long standing case. Steve was 54 at the time of the stroke and

CHAPTER FIVE   JOYCE

Laura was 53. He was 68 and she 67 at the time of our interview. Their family was the only one where memory and speaking had improved enough to allow for such an interview. His great improvements were laudable. He had survived for almost 1.5 decades since his stroke and memory loss condition began. Steve had improved over his 14 years and had much to add to the interviews about how he managed to do so.

Steve had run a successful electronics business prior to having his stroke and was the vice-president of the company. Prior to his stroke, he piloted an airplane on a regular basis, had excellent communication skills according to both he and his wife, and did international business for his company in Europe and the Middle East. All of that stopped after the memory loss condition began. Steve and Laura attributed his career loss to the memory loss for speaking and believed that Steve could have maintained his work otherwise.

Laura and Steve had two grown married sons, who were no longer in the home. For that reason, the parents described the impact upon these older children in the least devastating manner when compared with what I heard from the other families. However, even these adult children did attempt to help initially and remained involved thereafter. In fact, one of them even relocated moving ten minutes away from the parents' home.

The Eleven Concerns for Families after Memory Loss

The four interview discussions fell into 11 categories. The following chapter will review the families' own quotes and true stories. These occurred in the natural course of conversation with them about how

DON'T FORGET

language memory loss after stroke affected them personally.

1. Family expectations, understanding of language memory loss, and lack of education and information.

2. Perspective of families—Value given to communication and need for vocal memory loss rehabilitation.

3. Specific language memory, comprehension, speech, vocal losses, and memory improvements.

4. Speech/language therapy and other language memory loss improvement methods.

5. Fears.

6. Family living arrangements, adjustments, situations, and behaviors of children.

7. Role reversals and changes affecting family dynamics.

8. Marriage relationship changes.

9. Life style losses: Personality, social, financial, and career related.

10. Outside and professional health care and psychotherapeutic support.

11. Coping and psychological manifestations.

CHAPTER SIX

JOYCE

Chapter Six: The Families Speak to You Their Eleven Concerns after Memory Loss With 11 Subchapters

> *Subchapter VI-1: Family expectations, understanding of language memory loss, lack of education and information*

Not all hospitals offer stroke support or the needed medications to arrest stroke brain damage. Also, all hospitals do not offer information to the family or stroke victim explaining the nature of the memory loss problem when stroke or head injuries occur. The National Aphasia Association (NAA) holds support groups for language memory loss and is very desirous that families who want to begin to seek rehabilitation can do so as soon as possible. They recognize that early intervention is crucial to the success of the brain's recovery. Therefore, the NAA has long attempted to educate families and stroke victims offering assistance, brochures, public awareness and availability of NAA support groups. The NAA groups teach about language memory loss under the general heading of "aphasia" although many people have associated losses (Appendix A) who attend their group meetings. The NAA has surprisingly found that it is very difficult to distribute educational literature to inform memory loss parties and their families. In fact, the education of families affected by language memory loss from aphasia is not even permitted at every medical facility according to Penny Montgomery, the President of the NAA (personal communication, 1998).

DON'T FORGET

The families I interviewed expressed bewilderment that they received so little or no information about the memory loss before departing from the hospital. Each family came away with their own individual perspective, almost personally created, regarding the future outcomes for their aphasic family member and themselves. This makes about as much sense as going away from a hospital without knowing to wear a brace on a fractured leg or arm! Truly, allowing patients to fend for themselves and merely instructing them to call a speech pathologist when they get home does not meet the need. People are under stress during a family member's stroke and may simply forget this little understated one liner. The results can be serious and opportunities for recovery can slip away. When families of patients leave the hospital uninformed of the nature of this physical ailment, they may be led to believe treatment is unnecessary and that the disorder will correct itself. In the majority of aphasia cases, that is simply untrue and can cause the condition to stabilize untreated, like a broken arm would without being reset. Let me repeat, aphasia disorders require attention early on to be effectively healed. To not instruct families and patients of that fact seems criminal, yet, that is what is going on every day. The effect of this problem is reflected in the comments of these families.

CHAPTER SIX   JOYCE

Family One: Kay and Bob discuss expectations, understanding of language memory loss, lack of education and information

Kay discussed the discovery that Bob had a language memory loss called aphasia and what she believed and understood about his illness:

I don't remember when I first heard that word [aphasia]. I just knew he couldn't talk (652).

And Bob tried to tell me over the phone [from the hospital] that he wanted [pause] it sounded like he wanted his shaving things. And oh, I had to guess over the phone what he wanted. It was horrible (658-660).

He lost his speech . . . He was starting to pick up a lot of his words again and was doing pretty well. In fact, he was improving so fast that we [she and his children] thought, wow, he is going to be back to normal and back up on the air and everything, because he was in radio (17-21).

But I thought everything was going to be okay and he would, he would be okay again, you know, he'd be back on the air, it might take a little longer, but it was going to be okay (82-84).

Well, I just thought that he would get better. I thought until he died he would get better. Why did he die without getting better (737-738)?

From these comments, it appeared that Bob, Kay, and his children who lived with them, were uninformed about the memory loss condition from the onset of the stroke. Slowly, recognition of the implications on Bob's career and personal life began to set in. Kay was most aware of the impact of the disorder, but always believed Bob would improve and regain memory, speech, and health. Nonetheless, over time this family moved into a state of limbo, always hoping for recovery. At least, they kept up hope that way. Initially, Kay kept hoping for a complete recovery.

Family Two: Pam and Clay discuss expectations, understanding of language memory loss, lack of education and information

Pam described her experience of finding out that Clay could not talk and then explained how she came to understand the memory disturbance called aphasia and that it would become a part of their lives:

When I saw him I was really relieved because he looked perfectly fine. There was no obvious, to me, signs that he had anything wrong with him except when he tried to talk, nothing came out that was sensible. It was all gibberish. And he was certainly understanding at this time and by the look on my face that what he was saying wasn't making any sense. And he was trying to explain to me that his arm and his leg were numb (116-120).

CHAPTER SIX   JOYCE

Then we left the hospital knowing that he had aphasia [with the hospital personnel] not really explaining to either one of us what aphasia was . . .. Knowing that he had a stroke, not having any idea why he had this stroke, and being told, take him back to Maryland and he needs to see a neurologist, and he needs to work with a speech language pathologist. And no literature . . . And we left the hospital (129-136).

I would say all the way along from day one, it was just very scary to be told 'Well, your husband is going to have trouble talking for the rest so his life.' With no explanation, you know, 'Okay, he had a stroke, it hit this area of his brain,' and that's it [Laughing] (619-622).

And we got started that way. But the first six months we were told by the neurologist that was going to be the hardest time and by the end of that six months that would be what Clay would accomplish for probably for the rest of his life . . . [But that was] Absolutely not [the case]. And thank goodness because when that six months came and went, we were not at a very good place, because he was barely speaking. Most of his words still did not make any sense. And um, he still could not recognize or say, he could recognize them, but he couldn't say even the names of his children or myself (182-190).

Yeah. It is not until we got to our speech therapist, did she sit down, and open up some books and gave us some books, and said, 'This is what happened, read about this.' Of course, I could read it, and I would read it to Clay and try to explain. He had no idea what happened to him. He did not, until I would say, eight months post-stroke realize, he knew the word 'stroke,' he could not figure out what this word 'aphasia' was at all. He really did not comprehend what happened to him until eight months to a year post-stroke. Finally, he realized he wasn't worried about or dealing with stroke. He was dealing with aphasia. He had to live with aphasia for the rest of his life. So then, of course, when we got involved with Dr. Martha Taylor Sarno, she gave us a lot of information about aphasia. She founded the National Aphasia Association (NAA) because her father had a stroke and acquired aphasia and went through the same frustration. There was no information out there for families. So she decided at that time she was going to correct this problem (624-637).

We [NAA members] have tried to do that [educate aphasia families with bedside brochures]. It is pathetic. The response we get is, 'We cannot infringe on these peoples personal lives' . . . Their response is 'We can give them your number and it is up to them to call you.' And you know, you are so overwhelmed with everything that is happening and that gets tucked away in the back somewhere and you might think about it six months later or whatever or you might not think about it ever again (640-646).

That's the sad part, too [that people give up trying to improve]. That's why it would be very helpful if the hospitals could give them some information to go home with . . . That they could at least do something on their own as a family or have some beginning point (702-706).

CHAPTER SIX

JOYCE

Based on their own struggle, Pam and Clay became motivated to help other families with similar members to increase in their understanding of memory disorders through education. Pam expressed frustration that it is not normal procedure for a hospital to inform a person about the nature of their memory disorders. In essence, Pam and Clay did not understand very much about the disorder until later. Early on, they were told he only had six months to improve, which proved to be inaccurate. Afterwards, he continued to regain previous language memory and eventually became completely fine. Clay's and Pam's experiences and frustrations over being poorly informed by the health care system led them to become involved in the NAA, which, as previously stated, attempts to assist in educating and informing these families about the language memory loss disorder.

Family Three: Eve and Sarah discuss expectations, understanding of language memory loss, lack of education and information

Eve explained her confusion in understanding of what happened to her mother and how she came to know about the language memory loss aspect of the stroke:

"I knew she was brain damaged . . . Probably not til a month or so [when she learned about aphasia], a month, two months down the road. Well, actually, I might have learned it in the facility she was in. I don't remember exactly when I learned it. But I didn't learn it right away . . . Actually, in the hospital they kept on telling me, 'She'll probably be able to talk again.' And then awhile later they said, 'Maybe she won't ever talk again.' . . . Well the first week, [the doctor] he said 'She'd probably get her speech back.' Then by the second week, she was in the hospital for two weeks, he said, 'She might not ever talk again' (216-233).

They told me speech therapy [might help]. But, then it was never ordered for her. She never got it. She came home to my house and it was only with me after talking to the doctor for awhile, like two months down the road, she finally started speech therapy. Maybe a month and a half down the road. I don't remember exactly when, but it was a while (238-242).

[Also, when Eve was asked if she received any additional information, literature, or anything else about the nature of the language memory loss condition, either at the hospital or the facility that she stayed at once they realized, she replied that she had not received anything about her mother's speech, nor her language] (243-248).

From all appearances, Eve and Sarah were probably the most uninformed of all the patients and families thus far described. In addition, her mother's memory loss condition and loss of speaking ability was the most severe variety, global aphasia, the same as Clay's. The lack of ability to communicate with one another had serious ramifications for this mother-daughter relationship. However, according to the caregiver daughter, this particular health care system did not place

CHAPTER SIX   JOYCE

any emphasize on the value or importance of attempting to improve her mother's memory and ability to communicate during the most critical period for relearning in the case of neurological word loss, the first year.

In fact, before she left the hospital, the only information Eve received was that her mother might never speak again. Within only one week, her doctor changed his mind completely and reversed his initial prognosis that her speaking would get better to a prognosis that she would never speak again, all before she ever left the hospital! Phew! Now that's enough to make your head spin if your family just went through the devastation of a stroke. How does a doctor get to the point where he feels the necessity to blurt out such important information so casually and make such enormous shifts as he does?

This is what happens when insurance benefits are weak and there are not enough funds to procure proper assistance from speech and language therapists, who study the disorder and would have handled this differently. Even if Sarah never spoke again, the method of finding that out has a protocol to it that is no longer being followed with regularity, but ought to go back into effect everywhere to protect and service people properly.

Let's review how language memory loss was handled when insurance was not such an issue. First, at the hospital, a licensed speech and language pathologist made a diagnosis of the language memory loss problem. When the person returned home, another therapist followed up in the home or the family took the patient to an outpatient clinic. Then recommendations were made to increase speaking improvements. Then treatment was given until fairly normal memory and speech were restored.

Today, services run out way before a person has a chance to really improve to fairly normal levels. However, the protocol described above should at least be followed initially until the family has some understanding of the disorder and has learned the effect it will have on the patient and themselves. Then they could intelligently turn to other personally chosen methods that fit for their family as recommended by the speech and language professional or other memory-trained professional to help the aphasic person continue on the road to recovery. The speech and language pathologist could then visit for an occasional follow up to make recommendations. Even if patients and families must pay out of pocket for the therapist, such intermittent planning sessions would be far less expensive than continual ongoing therapy. However, depending on the language memory loss person, their level of difficulty and motivation for speaking again, families may wish to pay for the therapist to come and do ongoing therapy on occasion when the patient seems to be hitting a new plateau.

The long-term memory loss person, Steve, speaks about plateaus in the next dialogue. He made a strong point that he experienced many plateaus. Families who cannot afford any ongoing therapy services, if handled properly at the hospital, could at least begin to offer the language memory loss person assistance via computer, Internet, various books, music, and audiotaped reading material. Many advanced memory loss persons begin to know what helps them and will gladly begin to do

CHAPTER SIX   JOYCE

personal activities such as following along with an audio book or music while attempting to read or sing out loud. With just reasonable assistance and understanding that speaking practice is an exercise that will improve memory and speech, most aphasics will desire to find some personal methods for practicing the exercises of speaking, reading, or singing. Naturally, each person and family must decide what to do according to their own bent just as they would do exercises in a gym that suit them best. Sometimes people other than spouses, like friends or children help. Clay's children were able to do this.

Again, the reasons I offer these thoughts on non-conventional assistance is because the realities today are very different from what they used to be. Even the very difficult cases, like Sarah, got a good six months to try and speak again before talk of stopping for awhile came up. My experience with that method of handling neurological memory losses was very successful. Just as one attempts physical therapy for an arm or leg, whatever the outcome, giving the body a good college try and waiting hopefully for nerves and movement to come back, one ought to do the same for a cognitive memory loss. There are no guarantees with either therapy that normality will return. However, after making the attempt to follow a therapy regime, families can go on peacefully knowing they tried and did not just give up. Unfortunately, if there is little or no money left in the insurance plan to properly discern the dynamics of the memory loss, then the doctors are left to respond about future probabilities they cannot possibly know. At the same time, they must protect their liabilities, so what do they dare to say? Seen in that light, who can blame then if they give poor advice and little hope? The insurance companies are the ones who leave them holding the bag to give the answers to questions they do not always know with solutions all but pulled out from under them.

From reading Eve's quotes, you saw that the possibility for speech therapy was raised for Sarah. With that small hope given and no encouragement, Eve began the arduous task of attempting to obtain services for her mother during that acute critical period that followed. Though rehabilitation was once automatically ordered for someone like Sarah, that was not their experience. The hopelessness, negativity, and lack of some attention, input, or education from her medical community regarding the learning possibilities had an impact on both mother and daughter. Why? Well, like so many of us, they placed all their trust in their doctors, insurance, and the medical system. Consequently, they became hopeless, negative, and had little or no motivation to improve or begin the rehabilitation process necessary for success in such a case. That led to depression, fear, and worry. Afterward, when they felt they had failed to bring Sarah back to any intelligent memory and communication, Sarah could become one more case the system would point to as evidence that this disorder is hopeless. In fact, her health needs and their rights to be protected and properly informed were not met. Please do not tell me it is an invasion of a patient's rights for a hospital to properly inform, encourage, and assist people in receiving necessary medical treatment (Montgomery, P., personal communication, 1998)

CHAPTER SIX **JOYCE**

Family Four: Steve and Laura discuss expectations, understanding of language memory loss, lack of education and information

Steve and Laura discussed what they understood about his neurological memory loss at the time of the stroke and what they came to understand about the disorder over their 14 years post stroke and word loss onset with great interest and concern:

Steve: I remember that I couldn't speak. Cheryl, my daughter-in-law's sister made me a card with letters and some regularly used sentences and when they want to communicate me in the hospital, I could point to the letters and spell out a word or point to a sentence. Later on, they got me an electronic board from the hospital that you just press the letter and print on the screen (88-92).

I: So when did someone start talking about memory loss or the word aphasia?
Laura: No one ever did. His surgeon never told me. No one ever did, I knew it.
I: How did you figure it out?
Laura: Because I'd say, 'Okay, it's time for your shower.' And he'd be talking about eating.
I: So who used the word aphasia or explained language memory loss to you?
Laura: We didn't know the word aphasia until we joined the stroke club in Rochester and it was the social worker from the stroke club told me what he had (246-253).

DON'T FORGET

Laura: I didn't know what aphasia was in those days. So, I just thought he was doing it because he wanted to. But he would do anything I told him to do. Because he couldn't say "No." He didn't know. I'd put a toothbrush in his hand and he'd brush his teeth. In fact, I don't think he did realize what he was doing (283-286).

I: What did he [his doctor] say was wrong with him?
Laura: Well, he didn't say aphasia, but he said to me, "He doesn't understand what's going on"(388-390).

Laura: Dr G spoke at our stroke club on Saturday and he had the audacity to speak to about 85 people in our audience, we had a small turn out, thank God, and he said, "If you don't do it in two years, you're not going to get over it."
Steve: And he's wrong too.
Laura: So I said, "Well, look at my husband." And then he said, "Well, that's the exception." Isn't that awful?
Steve: They don't do studies for a long term. If they would follow me for instance from the day I had my stroke to today, they'd have a different attitude. Not only me, I tell you, I've seen hundreds of people that progress. It's true, they hit a plateau, but then they stay there so long and if they have the impetus and exercise and therapy they start moving up again. They get to another plateau, so there's a lot of plateaus in recovery. Now, I'm, 14 years since my stroke and I'm still improving, I'm still improving, not fast, very slow, but I'm still improving.
Laura: But his understanding, I call it, I would say a good two years before he started back talking in sentences,

CHAPTER SIX JOYCE

when I think about it, 'cause we went down to Grayson's to his birthday party and your sentence structure, you weren't really speaking that well there (595-612).

Steve: Some people believe that and stop getting better after six months because of that 'the doctor told me all I'll get as good as I'm going to get in six months' and after that that's it and they believe that and that's it. They don't even try anymore.
Laura: My husband does the stroke club paper.
I: So are you in favor of people having early education for their language memory loss?
Steve: It's important. Very important
Laura: Definitely and you know you have to keep talking to them. If you don't talk to them, they're not going to make progress. It's an absolute.
Steve: Very important. Everybody should have the information of exactly what's wrong with them. It's best to be honest and tell them you don't know how much they're going to improve. You really don't know. Some people don't, I don't know why. Either they gave up or they just don't have the ability to improve. But other people improve.
Laura: But he knew what he wanted to say, it just wouldn't come out.
Steve: And it's wrong for any doctor to tell a person, "Oh, this is all you're going to improve in this time frame, after that forget it." That's wrong.
I: So then the other thing you're saying is that people need to hear from other memory loss persons?
Steve: Right, yes.
Laura: Like he keeps telling this man, "Look, if I can get

DON'T FORGET

the use of my arm back, you can." And hopefully he will (615-637).

    Clearly, Steve and Laura came to understand a great deal about memory loss that they learned through life's trials and errors over time. Steve maintained that he was still improving his speech and memory of language and was disgruntled with therapists and a system that stops the rehabilitative process too quickly and at the first sign of the patient leveling off and not increasing in language learning. As a therapist, I obviously concur and feel his frustration as well. When you know you will not be given the necessary time to accomplish the recovery task with the patient, as a therapist, it becomes difficult to get excited about doing two or three days or weeks of therapy with them. However, in the future, it may be that the therapist will do some therapy and then more planning with the family about their particular mode of moving forward and succeeding. History proves language memory loss by aphasia can be helped much more than it is today. If so, money and insurance must step out of the way. Therapists and families must become creative together when that is possible and families are willing. Some say family members cannot do this work together. I say that depends on the family. If the family or couple cannot work together then maybe the way will open for a child, sibling, or friend to help occasionally or take turns with one another. Stimulation, not perfection, is key.

CHAPTER SIX **JOYCE**

Reflections on family expectations, understanding of language memory loss, lack of education and information

From the quotes about the families' understanding and expectations of neurological memory loss of words, one realizes, they were unclear about what was going on from the moment the aphasic patient began to exhibit difficulty talking. The families moved into limbo-like states and became confused about whether the disorder could be helped or not. When the families operated by believing that improvement could occur and made steps toward that goal, they appeared more contented in spite of this neurological memory loss for words. Laura also received more cooperation from medical professionals. This was possibly related to having positive direction and goals to work toward together. They also had the additional comfort of knowing that they were doing all that could be done to heal the damage of the neurological word losses. That helped them emotionally and benefited them even when the recovery was imperfect.

Naturally, during the early stages, families knew the least. In the interview with Eve, I heard expressions of the greatest frustration, confusion about the future, and fear over whether the family members would all be contented in their ongoing relationships. Families in the latter stages believed that early-on coping must be established: All parties need to move in a direction that can positively influence memory and communication. Any assistance from anyone leading to improved language skills was received gratefully. This was especially true during that critical period for relearning, the first few months to the first years after the stroke. Some of the families interviewed worked toward improvement without professional advice, and instead, allowed their personal experience to guide them. Of course, other families seemed rather stymied and gave up in ways that might not have occurred with support, encouragement to try, education, and/or information about all the possibilities of recovery.

In review, according to all available research about recovery from language memory loss, one ought to begin retraining as soon as one is medically able to maximize that best time for potential relearning. Though each case represented here held many variables affecting the final outcome, potential, and future, ultimately, the medical community possessed the ability to inform the families of language memory loss and to allow them to attempt the best possible results. To leave them uninformed was non-responsive to their needs.

Furthermore, despite receiving their treatments in a country with access to the highest state of the art of medical information, the participants in my study reported being uninformed and uneducated about the disorder which had become the focal point of their lives. Like it or not, memory loss is a life changing force. Some method of informing or educating them appeared to be lacking allowing them to choose whatever rehabilitation style would best fit their family. Clearly, when there are memory improvements, less stress and better relationships occur in the families decreasing the mental health issues.

CHAPTER SIX JOYCE

> *Subchapter VI-2: Perspective of families— Value given to communication and need for vocal memory loss rehabilitation*

Closely related to understanding and the expectations for the future follows another area of importance that the families each talked about, the importance of memory and good communication before the stroke and the need for improvement afterwards. Eve described her mother as a very quiet person before her stroke, while the men discussed used all their communication talents regularly and in every area of life. Naturally, caregivers watched them and expressed that the person experienced great losses across the board. Even Eve, who described Sarah as non-talkative, expressed the strong affects of her mother's memory loss on the social and family ties. Families knew the person's communication style pre-stroke, so this evoked interesting discussions.

Family One: Bob and Kay discuss the value given to communication and need for vocal memory loss rehabilitation

Kay explained how Bob's communication ability was the most important aspect of his life and work next to his relationships with God and his family:

[If Bob had a stroke but still could have spoken] Oh, I think Bob's voice was everything to him. Next to his wife, and his family, and his God, you know, his children. I mean he loved radio. So he could have been in radio and it wouldn't have mattered if he was in a wheelchair, but he could have been on radio. You know, Franklin Delano Roosevelt could run the White House during the war, within his wheelchair, Bob could have done it . . . But his voice, I think he lost a lot of self-confidence (489-493).

He loved it. He loved it. He loved radio. He loved radio. He just loved it (370).

Well, his speaking voice was a gift, but he had an ability to read the bible that well, Helen Hayes said it, "He had the definitive voice to read the bible." He sent her his tapes one time . . . And I still have that. That was nice that she wrote that letter to him (318-322).

Lorne Greene had an acting school in Ottawa and Bob went to his school. And [Bob] learned how to use his voice to be expressive and you know. Of course, when he got to Wheeling, West Virginia, he was doing Loretta Lynn, a lot of people, the Osmond Brothers, I can't think of anymore right off hand, but these were all people that he was their boss; because he ended up working on Jamboree USA, and he just loved it (356-362).

Okay. Well he had . . . When he was a little boy he had a stuttering problem. And his parents took him to doctors and everything and nobody seemed to do very much to [sic] him . . . And the first verse he ever read in the bible was in Mark 7, 'and they suddenly brought unto him a man with a speech impediment. And Jesus healed him.' And so, he thought, 'well, if Jesus could do that for him then he could heal me, too.' And he read more in this bible that night and he ended up inviting Jesus to come into his heart as his savior. And told the Lord that, if he would give him his speech, he would read the bible to as many people as would listen to him (272-296).

For Bob and Kay, speaking was of extremely high value. This memory loss person's life was wrapped up in the communication field. The use of his memory skills, language and voice represented who he was as a person. Even his understanding of his spirituality and relationship with God was bound up in his ability to recall language effectively for public speaking purposes. Loss of his superb communication abilities affected every area of his personality, and subsequently, the lives of his wife and children.

Family Two: Pam and Clay discuss the value given to communication and need for vocal memory loss rehabilitation

Pam described a tenacity, intensity, and importance that both she and her husband held regarding his communicative abilities during the three-year period in which he successfully attempted to regain his language memory and speaking ability after acquiring global aphasia, the most severe language memory loss:

[If Clay had a stroke, but still could have spoken] . . .Well, I think after he got better he was able to explain that to him the worst part of it all was not being able to speak. Because he had worked. He was not a college graduate. He went to college dropped out and joined the

DON'T FORGET

Air Force. Got out of the Air Force and well in the Air Force, decided he needed to educate himself because he felt like he had very definite goals for himself and he knew he wasn't going to reach those goals unless, number one, he improved his communication skills. So he started a personal project for himself that required so many new words being learned every month and he joined Toastmaster's and different things like that; to make himself improve on speaking in public and also presenting himself to banks and companies. And he worked himself up the ladder. And he just worked very hard, but he did say that the aphasia was the hardest thing to deal with (504-514).

He grew up, his parents were both deaf, so he grew up in a deaf home, so he knew how important communication was and he always has felt, ever since he was a little boy, that you had to be well versed in this world to get where you wanted to go. And I think that was his mother and father influencing him because of their deafness (514-519).

So it was very, very big impact on him when he lost his ability to speak. And it was just, he was so determined at 44 years old to get that speech back. Not only for himself, but for his family and for his whole world. So he set out this project and he conquered it [Laughing] (521-524).

Speech therapy did last a year. He went on for two years, which we did pay out of our pocket, but it was worth it, it was important, it was something he had to do. And there

CHAPTER SIX   JOYCE

was no question that that was going to be done. So financially it really didn't change our situation that much, thank goodness (550-554).

Well, my husband was just determined to get better about this aphasia and he just set out to find out as much as he could about this word, and just started looking up aphasia every place, everywhere he could possible think that he might be able to get any information. Just through word of mouth (565-568).

He heard about an association that was just forming in New York and it was called the National Aphasia Association, and he called the president and went up to New York and met her personally; Dr. Martha Taylor Sarno . . . He just expressed his sincere desire to get involved and that's how we got involved. And she informed him at that time that there are support groups for people who have aphasia as well as their caregivers. A lot of them are called stroke groups, but she made sure he understood that he had to find one with people who had aphasia that attended (572-580).

    Clay placed very high values on his recall for speaking abilities. He was a self-starter and highly motivated individual whose deaf parents had clearly taught him that his ability to communicate was extremely important. Therefore, when Clay was inflicted with the most severe form of aphasia, global aphasia, he set out on a mission to change his situation and regain his memory and communication skills. Speech therapy did help him improve his communication, but did not lead him on to the level of improvement that he eventually gained through his own search and motivation. Another helpful aspect of his memory loss was that he had none of the other usual bodily impairments that often accompany stroke to distract him from his goals. His only stroke consequence was pure global aphasia, the language memory disability.

Family Three: Eve and Sarah discuss the value given to communication and need for vocal memory loss rehabilitation

Eve expressed her frustration over the change in her mother as related to the value of lost communication:

[If Sarah had a stroke but could still speak] . . . It would be much better. I could have a better relationship with her I think. Cause I think that's her problem for her. She is very angry. She is very depressed. I imagine she's got to be frustrated with this. I already pray to God every single night if only one miracle could happen just give her back her speech. Because at least then she could tell us what she feels like. I know she in unhappy and all that. But at least, well then, we could have, we could communicate differently. It's like having my mother back (193-199).

She only wants me to do for her and that is it. And I think my mother also believes that she is not that tough to do, it's not a lot of work. I don't know what she's really thinking cause she can't tell me (363-365).

CHAPTER SIX   **JOYCE**

Just I mean she is my mother, but I don't, because I talk to her now, but I can't have a conversation with her. Before if I had problems, I would be able to talk to her about them. I can't do that anymore, you know what I'm talking about? Because she really doesn't understand, and if she does she can't give me any feedback. She can't tell me (169-171).

The value of communication for Eve and Sarah was expressed in terms of the frustration that occurred during the care giving episodes between them. Here, Sarah's lack of comprehension during basic activities of daily living added another barrier to an already difficult situation. The dire element was that Eve and Sarah could no longer communicate with each other though they were so very close throughout her pre-stroke life, and when Eve was a child and Sarah was her caretaker. Eve prayed only one prayer every single night, if only one miracle could happen, it would be to give her mother's speech back.

Family Four: Steve and Laura discuss the value given to communication and need for vocal memory loss rehabilitation

Steve and Laura expressed the importance to them for Steve to be able to speak after his stroke and aphasia:

I: Now what would have been different if you had the stroke and all the other problems, but could still speak as before?
Laura: He probably could have gone back to work.

DON'T FORGET

Steve: Oh, yeah (333-336).

I: So tell me about your speech problem?
Steve: Well, that aphasia was one of the things that prevented me from going back to work, because if nobody can understand you.
Laura: You couldn't walk very well.
I: But if you hadn't been able to walk, but had been able to talk?
Steve: I could have gone back to work.
I: Even with the leg not working?
Steve: I'd have used a wheelchair or a scooter (333-344).

Again, as in each of the cases, Steve and Laura address the dramatic influence of being unable to recall for communication as the overwhelming stroke difficulty after time has set in and life needs to return to a place of balance with friends and work.

Reflections on value given to communication and need for vocal memory loss rehabilitation

All participants' lives revealed the incredible truth that communication is normally highly valued among human beings. Their utter and complete involvement with one another and their methods for living required a constant intertwining of communication and recall. Those individuals who valued communication the most highly and were most invested in recouping pre-illness communication states worked hard to improve. Each person responded uniquely regarding the importance of communication and how life would be different if their loved one had a stroke, but was still able to speak and recall words as before the stroke. In that regard, the value of memory and being able to speak even with other physical losses was expressed.

At times, I attempted to recall my own experiences with communication and memory loss, but can only say mine are only as similar as tying a scarf over one's eyes to discover the difficulties of blindness when compared to these losses. Even the metaphor I used expressing the difficulties of speaking in a country where a foreign language is used can only be considered as a comparison for learning and for purposes of shifting attitudes and vantage points.

DON'T FORGET

> *Subchapter VI-3: Specific language, memory, comprehension, speech, vocal losses and improvements*

Naturally, the type and severity level of the memory loss affected certain specific speech, language, memory, and vocal manifestations in each individual patient. To understand how the impediments influenced the person and family, first, it would help to know the symptoms (see Appendix A & B). Also, each person's prior life and use of communication in relationships was challenged uniquely in specific ways ordained by their disorder. Though similarities will always occur across cases, there will also be important distinctive features specific to each case as well.

Family One: Kay and Bob discuss specific language, memory, speech, vocal losses and improvements

Here Kay described problems, which occur when aggramaticism, anomia, and dyslexia are prominent in the language memory loss person's aphasia (Appendix A):

Oh please! He had to have speech therapy and he couldn't recall words really fast. I mean he would get the "church," the "school," cause he worked in Christian radio, but it was educational Christian radio. But it was located in the church building. So he would get the "church," the "school," and the "hospital" all mixed up. Sometimes he'd call the "church" the "hospital." Sometimes, and "he's" and "she's", you know. He'd be talking about like a speech therapist, who was a woman and say "he." You know, I mean it was sort of like, it was really hard for him. He was never able to be spontaneous on the air anymore. And his reading, I think it affected his eyesight because instead of double spacing his words in capital letters for reading, he had to triple space it, just to get the words in. Sometimes the words would all flow together. So, reading was really hard for him, too. So I think it affected his eyesight (382-393).

And you know I knew the quality of my husband's voice. And he didn't hear it, but I could tell that when he taped things the quality was not as good as it had been before. And so I think he lost some ability to hear because he used to be able to tell when it was not exactly right. And now I could tell things that he wasn't picking up. So that made me feel kind of bad because I knew he had lost so much . . . (395-399).

Because he loved the way his voice was when he got a cold; cause it was that old deep resonance again. And he lost some of the resonance when . . . (1087-1089).

After the stroke he never did a live interview. There was no way (414).

And after that it was just, you know, he, sometimes when they had the big concerts, he would get in front of the audience for a couple minutes and he would get nervous and lose it. Where as, before he never got nervous (423-425).

DON'T FORGET

Bob's memory loss symptoms revealed themselves in grammatical errors, loss of easy access to his vocabulary, and visual disturbances. The reading problems, vocal quality, and word finding impairments during spontaneous communication upset his radio work and impeccable communication style. Other persons with a similar type of aphasia, but less dependence upon communication to earn a living might have been less affected by the same mild to moderate level of disorder.

Family Two: Clay and Pam discuss specific language, memory, speech, vocal losses and improvements

Pam described Clay's communication as it occurred during the various stages he passed through starting from the onset and moving to the third year post-language memory loss:

There was no obvious to me signs that he had anything wrong with him except when he tried to talk, nothing came out that was sensible. It was all gibberish. And he was certainly understanding at this time and by the look on my face that what he was saying wasn't making any sense (116-119).

Absolutely not. [States that Clay's rehabilitation potential was not nearly reached six months post-aphasia onset as so many aphasia families are told]. And thank goodness because when that six months came and went, we were not at a very good place, because he was barely speaking. Most of his words still did not make any sense. And um,

CHAPTER SIX JOYCE

he still could not recognize or say, he could recognize them, but he couldn't say even the names of his children or myself . . . He called me "Paint" for I guess almost a year. It was maybe not quite that long. For the first six months, he had what they refer to as global aphasia in where he could not read, speak, write, or comprehend much (186-194).

The first three years were the hardest, I think. The first six months were absolutely the hardest (171-172).

Three years post stroke he was talking very well. He always did talk slower because we had lived in the south for quite a while and so he really was the type of person who spoke very carefully and thought first before he spoke. So if you didn't know anything had happened to him, you wouldn't have even realized it (210-214).

But thank goodness, in his case, it did start switching back. After the first year, he really started improving by leaps and bounds (400-401).

And like I said by three years you could hardly tell (403).

Clay's speech and language were very severely impaired at the time of his stroke indicating global language memory loss. Pam explained that he could not communicate at all the first six months. Then changes occurred that allowed him to go back to work part-time. By a year later, he began to understand in ways he had not before. Three years later, she attests repeatedly throughout her story that you would not have known that two and one-half years before he was unable to speak when he was six months into the disorder. This speech description clarified the importance of recognizing the amazing wide gamut of possibilities for these patients and consequently, the families. The value of hopefulness became evident when one had a severe type of aphasia language memory loss and could not speak for the first six months or even the first year. Even if full recovery had not occurred, the lack of hope if there was even a chance at recovery appeared more devastating. Many professionals would not counsel such a family as Clay's and Pam's to continue this pursuit and yet, they achieved their goal. Placed in this same circumstance, wouldn't you want your own family and many families you know to make similar attempts for one another? Come on. Isn't this life anyway? What else do we all have going that is so important if not help one another?

Family Three: Eve and Sarah discuss specific language, memory, speech, vocal losses and improvements

Eve commented on how her mother, Sarah, communicated after the stroke, not through speaking, but through a changed nature. Though mother and daughter learned a few methods to compensate for the problems, their circumstance remained difficult, particularly because Sarah no longer understood what Eve was saying during the acute phase:

I don't know what she's really thinking, cause she can't tell me (364-365).

CHAPTER SIX JOYCE

Yeah, and she refuses to help herself at all. Okay, she won't do anything . . . She wants me to do it all for her . . . I said to her, "Now, I can't do this anymore . . . You are going to have to do a lot for yourself. You obviously can't." I said, "You better start thinking about who's going to come into this house to help me help you." . . . And I said to her, "If you're willing for me, I will give her a call back [previous nursing assistant]. Hopefully she didn't get another job, yet, and she might be willing to come back and give you another try." So she yelled at me, waving her hands like to say if I'd 'go get her "yes – no" papers' because she because she [repeats self] gets such confusion on when she sees the words. And she pointed to 'yes,' I can go call. I said to her, "Are you going to be nice to her now, tomorrow? I don't want you to be nasty to her. You've got to be nice." And she did the same thing and said, "Yes." So at this, I went and called the lady back. Luckily enough she didn't have another job . . .(360-431).

This one [nursing assistant] is willing to stay because she realized it's not something directly against her, it's just her condition. It's causing her to be this mean ornery person . . . I've come along. I'm learning that a lot of her what she does is not in her own control, because this was never my mother (432-433).

So she would never, never do anything that would harm me, so the fact that she is not accepting these women. I realize that it is completely out of her control (439-441).

Just I mean she is my mother, but I don't, because I talk

to her now, but I can't have a conversation with her. Before if I had problems, I would be able to talk to her about them. I can't do that anymore, you know what I'm talking about? Because she really doesn't understand, and if she does she can't give me any feedback. She can't tell me (169-171).

Sarah exhibited some other symptoms frequently seen especially with poor comprehension ability: A loss of control and a change in emotionality and personality. Here, neurological disturbances were accompanied by a lack of hope for recovery, personal frustration, and changes in behavior. These feelings and behavior changes made perfect sense as they related to the real possibilities that Eve noted for Sarah of permanently losing one's former self and being locked inside her body without a voice.

Family Four: Steve and Laura discuss specific language, memory, speech, vocal losses and improvements

Steve and Laura expressed what they believed was Steve's specific disability in speaking and using language after his stroke:

Steve: Well, at first, I couldn't do anything really. I had no speech really. I had a very cool understanding, you know, I used the board, you know, to point out words, but very few.

CHAPTER SIX   JOYCE

I: So after a year went by, how were your speech, language, and voice by then?
Steve: Oh, I think by a year it was a lot better. And then I think I was getting speech therapy (189-194).
Laura: When they would talk to him in the hospital, they thought he was mentally unbalanced because and you remember he had a stoma [surgical hole in neck], too (218-219).

Steve: Sometimes it's very difficult to talk. Sometimes I have to think harder to get the words I want to say and I still do today, but I'm a 1000% better than I used to be, that's for sure. So I know I'm not 100% right (577-579).

Laura: But his understanding, I call it, that was really his aphasia, I would say a good two years before he started back talking in sentences, when I think about it (609-610).

After fourteen years, this couple recalled the many and varied stroke problems including first and foremost the aphasia language memory loss problem. This was accompanied by dysarthria, a motor disturbance, which slows down pronunciation, and dysphagia which creates difficulty in swallowing. These problems overlapped making it even more difficult for Steve to communicate. The strong impression the combined problems left revealed the significant impact the disorder made upon their couple-hood and lives.

DON'T FORGET

Reflections on specific language, memory, speech, vocal losses and improvements

In this section on communication changes, (see Appendix A), the families reported how the various forms of memory loss manifested themselves in their family member's communication. The description of unique features in each person afflicted lent each case its individuality and showed the understanding the reporting family member eventually gained about the specifics of the language memory disorder, the loss of word finding ability, and neurological communication losses in general. Though this section did not yield diagnoses (Appendix B), the impact on the family is recognized more clearly in terms of their narrative descriptions, which add personal, non-professional vitality. In that regard, these expressions of the disabling aspects offered the family lens much clearer than a professional opinion in many respects. As family members seldom have opportunities to give such descriptions, these comments offer their enlightenment. These conversations also open up possibilities for ways to intervene. Therapeutic interventions develop out of discussions such as these that could assist any professional health care therapist to be more helpful in the future and could also help family members in deciding what to practice and stimulate, in essence, guided by the family member with the loss.

CHAPTER SIX   JOYCE

> ➤ *Subchapter VI-4. Speech/language therapy and other language memory loss improvement methods*

According to research, the language improvements that occur during memory loss reduction require time, patience, persistence, and new speech, language, and vocal habits. All of these aid in the rehabilitation of skills and optimally used become part and parcel of the way of life.

Family One: Kay and Bob discuss speech/language therapy and other language memory loss improvement methods

Kay was somewhat discouraged in her attempts to assist Bob in continuing his work. When she worked with him herself, she felt like a teacher with an unwilling pupil:

I thought it was in his head because he didn't want to do speech, but it wasn't. His arm really did hurt, cause it was really frozen (1229-1231).

I just felt like he should work harder. I mean when you're the wife on the other end and you don't know what is going to happen with your future or the future of your family, I mean you just think, 'Why don't you work every minute of the day on this, Bob' (1248-1249)?

And he didn't want to work for me at nights either

sometimes. I had to fight with him, not fight, but cajole and encourage, motivate. It was almost like teaching another class (1252-1254).

"Honey, maybe you should go for speech again or maybe you should get another speech therapist. Or honey, why aren't you singing? Do you sing in the car anymore?" Because he loved the way his voice was when he got a cold; cause it was that old deep resonance again. And he lost some of the resonance when . . . (1085-1088).

And I was making up lesson plans for people for things to do with Bob during the day, and then I helped him at night. And he worked probably better for everyone else but me (590-592).

Well, I encouraged him till the day he died (1083).

Well, I just thought that he would get better. I thought until he died he would get better. Why did he die without getting better (737-738)?

Though Bob coveted his former communication abilities, he only seemed able to work on his recovery at a pace that suited his personality and health after his stroke. In some respects, he was a little embarrassed by it. To Kay, his attempts at recovery were less then she had hoped for. To Bob, they may have been all he could give before he died of heart attack six years later. Kay clearly inspired Bob to continue even though he was weaker than he had been pre-stroke. Her persistence may have given

CHAPTER SIX   **JOYCE**

him the motivation and improved the quality of his final years by adding the lovely quality of hopefulness she had for him that surely he would become his old self once again. However, he came very far and was able to continue managing the radio station until the day he died.

Family Two: Clay and Pam discuss speech/language therapy and other language memory loss improvement methods

Pam described the unfolding of their family project:

The speech therapist was so good. She worked with him everyday, five days a week. Some days it was only 15 minutes, some days it was an hour depending on his strength and his, he got tired a lot at that point (194-197).

And he did continue to have speech therapy every day and then it cut back to four times a week, three times a week and so on and so forth until the end of the third year the speech therapist was seeing him about once a month just to check in with him. And finally, she said I really can't do this anymore. You really are fine and he got the point (195-198).

The girls, well, the five year old, was learning how to read in kindergarten. And of course, the four-year old was right behind, and she was interested in that, too. And they would read their books to Clay (291-293).

And then Clay would try to read the sentences back or the

DON'T FORGET

word. This wasn't right away, but later down the road, and it really became like part of his homework. It was fine with them because they were helping daddy to get better, and so they really enjoyed that (295-300).

The kids, they really did join all together in helping in one way or another. Now when my oldest daughter realized that he was getting better, then she too joined in, in helping with his homework, because he did have homework from this therapist every time he met with her, and we would all help with that. She became very active in her role, too, as a teenager, helping him out (314-318).

My teenager enjoyed doing that with him [driving] and testing him to make sure he could read the signs (325-326).

Ask them [speech therapists] for as much help before your relationship ends for the future time that you are going to be having to work with the person with aphasia, because they will be able to hopefully send you in the right direction (715-718).

And also I've told them, don't go every time if you can't do it, but go periodically to the speech therapy session so you know what they do. Some spouses or caregivers feel like this is their free time and it is important to have free time, too. But you need to know what's going on in speech therapy if you are going to have to be doing it later down the road . . . But it would be good for families to be

CHAPTER SIX　　　　　　　　　　JOYCE

able to have an on going relationship or contact point with some kind of speech therapist I feel (720-735).

This couple was fortunate to be able to use a speech therapist for three years, and I am certain that without that level of interest, this man could not have come as far as he did. In addition, the entire family recognized the value of assisting Clay's memory and communication personally. Even his children worked with him regularly to improve. In the end, the husband and wife went beyond their own personal project and began to work in the support groups of the National Aphasia Association. Frustration over their own need for assistance motivated them to participate in offering support to other families throughout the United States. Clay and Pam were obviously never casual observers in their lives. Fortunately, their pre-stroke life style caused them to become part of this great ongoing task and lend their voices of experience to others. This family, headed up by Clay, set out to meet the challenges of healing and treating aphasia language memory loss by making it an on-going family project that then became part of all their lives. In the end, they conquered his language memory loss together.

Family Three: Eve discusses speech/language therapy and other language memory loss improvement methods

Eve described her experiences communicating with her mother using methods she devised and further revealed her difficulties obtaining ongoing professional speech services:

DON'T FORGET

And she's learned how to use the telephone to call me and its programmed to call my cell phone . . . Yeah. I always say to her on the phone, if I hear, "Oh God, Oh God," I know it's like, you know it's like, everything is okay. If I hear 'bah, bah, bah,' like I say, it's an emergency and I'll call 911. You know, something like that. But basically, it's just her, as long as it comes up on my caller I.D. on my cell phone I would either just get home right away; because I'm never usually more than 10 minutes away from the house. Or if I feel it's something else, I would just dial 911 for her. And the telephone is like pre-coded. I have it color coded, so she doesn't get confused and she knows exactly what buttons to press. And plus all the buttons . . . Even if she pushes the wrong one, all the buttons are made to go to my cell phone. Because I have one special button coded so she knows to push that one but if she misses and pushes the wrong one, it still calls my cell phone, because everyone has been done to the cell phone (38-52).

So she yelled at me, waving her hands like to say if I'd go get her "yes – no" papers because she because she gets such confusion on when she sees the words. And she pointed to 'yes,' I can go call (416-419).

They told me speech therapy [might help]. But, then it was never ordered for her. She never got it. She came home to my house and it was only with me after talking to the doctor for a while, like two months down the road, she finally started speech therapy. Maybe a month and a half

CHAPTER SIX   JOYCE

down the road. I don't remember exactly when, but it was a while (238-242).

He ordered it [physical, occupational, speech therapy] again. He keeps on ordering it, but it hasn't started. I'm supposed to give him a call this afternoon to see what's going on . . . the insurance company allows two weeks at a time so when it runs out he [the physician] orders it again . . . So well then sometimes we have a lapse of a month in between and then they'll get started again . . . I think it's the insurance fault. I don't think it's the doctor. I think it's the insurance . . . He'll just say that he'll put the order in. Then he'll tell us, if you don't hear from them within a few days, call me again and he'll call it in again . . . And some times . . . he has to call in an order to get an order to go . . . It's almost a week away. I haven't heard from the occupational therapist or physical therapist yet. . . I have to call him again and let him [physician] know that I haven't heard [from] them. I give them a few days, but like I said, today, I was going to call again (608-630).

    Eve and Sarah came up with some of their own fail-safe devices to assist themselves in ways a speech therapist would. Her mother learned to call her on the telephone by pressing a button and responded to written words on a paper indicating "yes" or "no." However, actual therapy services were sporadic and only lasted for a few months with several breaks in the services according to Eve. Indeed, Eve expressed frustration in obtaining services in all the therapeutic venues in her attempts to find help for her mother's speech and other stroke ailments. In spite of her attempts, this family exemplified one put off too many times, and as a result, began to give up hope for improvement, a sad state. Their problem of being put off then became a related issue for this patient's prognosis. In other words, the medical community cannot separate themselves from the outcomes for the family by failing to provide services and needed information and educational resources. The very fact that they do not contribute such data to the family system is a factor that will insure the patient of the detrimental outcome and remove many possibilities research has shown could occur to improve aphasia.

Family Four: Steve and Laura discuss speech/language therapy and other language memory loss improvement methods

This couple, who had been dealing with the results of stroke for 14-years, had an educated, interesting perspective about methods for assisting and dealing with the speech and language memory losses. Indeed, the aphasic patient himself became impassioned as he went over his thoughts about how his language memory improved over the years:

Laura: Or he wanted me to do something and he couldn't get that across to me and I'd sit down and say, "Well, let's go through this again." And I would take clues. In fact, his doctor said I was the only one who could understand him, even when he was in the hospital (96-99).

CHAPTER SIX   **JOYCE**

Steve: One of my partners, we used to manufacture special purpose computers, so he brought me a computer at home, and I was using that and eventually my cognitive memory came back.
I: Eventually, how long was that?
Steve: About a year or more (103-106).

Steve: So he borrowed the computer and, you know, I couldn't read, you know, apparently I couldn't recognize words. When we put our program up where it would talk back to me, I'd type a word and it would tell me whether it was correct.
Laura: In the beginning you and I typed in, I'd put the words on your screen (111-115).

Laura: If they have aphasia, get yourself a computer and sit down with your mate that can't speak if the words are not matching what you say.
Steve: What also helps is 'talking books.' I didn't have it then
I: You're talking about audiocassette books to get language skills back?
Steve: What they can do as well, I can't because my hand shakes too much, but they can follow that in a regular book, too, which means visually they can read individually. They can read along (450-456).

I: You felt he was finished, how much more do you think he could have used?
Laura: Another year.
I: They stopped way too soon.
Steve: Everything.

DON'T FORGET

Laura: Now with balanced budget act . . . everything has been cut. You can't even get those services (461-466).

Steve: The more you get, [speech therapy] the better off you are. Whether you hit a plateau or not for a while. And that's what's wrong with therapists, they say, "Oh," as soon as you hit a plateau, "it's over."
Laura: But that's because they're not allowed to give anymore that's how much [money] there is [for it] (630-633).

Laura assisted Steve in his speech and memory work, and Steve was a very willing participant in this process. Steve had done a great deal of the work himself and was proud of how he had plateaued and improved, plateaued and improved, plateaued and improved over 14 years. Steve felt therapists give up too easily at the plateau levels, which occur and physicians do not realize that the plateaus could eventually change and a memory loss patient could hit several more learning curves over the lifetime of the disorder.

Reflections on speech/language therapy and other language memory loss improvement methods

Without the needed drill, practice, and work required to improve memory of language, all of the families and patients in the study might have been as frustrated as the new arrivals, Kay and Sarah. Instead, each one worked out their situation based on their own creativity and motivation. Clay, for example, was young enough and healthy enough to make his recovery happen

CHAPTER SIX — JOYCE

and to pay speech therapists out of pocket payments, commonly known as fee for services, after his insured speech therapy services ran out. Also, he did not have to pay additionally for physical or occupational therapists to assist him with those associated ailments as he had none. Steve and his wife creatively continued to invent methods for his improvement on their own for 14 years. Bob had insurance from his managerial radio position for his speech therapy for over three years, which made it easy for him to continue receiving services until then. After that time, he and Kay and members of the church worked with Bob.

Speech therapy services have diminished, but most of the families in my study devised some therapeutic methods or strategies of their own to cope, compensate, and reduce the aphasia language memory loss problems. Those families had just enough therapy to know they wanted to continue something on their own because it was making a difference in their lives. Some of the ideas came from their speech therapy experiences. However, the families needed motivation and a sense of purpose or solid reasoning to continue striving to improve when services stopped or were insufficient. Therefore, at the very least, the patients and involved family members needed to be informed and educated about the possibilities and probabilities one has to accept with this disorder. If there are no funds for speech therapy, at least consult with one or with others who can give caregiver support. Therapists who follow up can solidify maintenance of the gains fought for and can attend to the person's readiness for future improvements and possibilities.

DON'T FORGET

The present medical climate in which standoffishness about rehabilitation has become commonplace has serious implications in affecting future outcomes for these patients' prognoses. If the medical community fails to provide either needed services or at least information to families of language memory loss patients, it cannot exempt itself from liability for those patients who might have improved. Medical research has long shown that positive outcomes are possible and often probable for those neurologically damaged from memory losses. Patients who are assisted in the endeavor of relearning language after aphasia memory loss, more often than not, do improve given the correct amounts of service necessary to the severity of the disorder. Informing people of this truth legally should not and does not appear to be an option for medical practitioners and therapists who work with this population. Though it has been overlooked in the present insurance climate, according to the information garnered in my discussions with family members, this must change and it is only a matter of time before families will stand up and demand changes in the protocol for these services.

CHAPTER SIX   **JOYCE**

> ### *Subchapter VI-5. Fears*

Fears for the future emanated from some families and extended beyond future possibilities moving into actual losses in health, relationships, career and work. One upsetting feature of the families' fears occurred when the added possibility of losing the aphasic person to death due to their health existed. The differences in the expression of their fears unfolded in each case differently and depended upon whether their case was acute, chronic, or the patient had already died.

Family One: Kay and Bob discuss fears

Kay ideally expected Bob to go on living and working as a communicator. However, at the time of the interview, Bob was deceased. From Kay's story, it appeared that during his recovery period he attempted to live up to her ideal and make it his own as well. However, the fear of falling from that state added pain to their situation at the start of the stroke and during the last years of his life:

I think he was afraid he was going to lose his job. And his boss, his immediate boss, spoke to him about hurrying up and getting well. And his doctor called the boss that was higher than his boss and said, "How can you hurry a person getting well" (458-462)?

He ended up with a frozen shoulder. And he wasn't walking for the first couple of weeks . . . I didn't really worry about that. But what really concerned me was his speech, because he was a radioman, and he didn't seem to be coming out of this stroke like he came out of the other one . . .(76-80).

And Bob was crying in the car. He was so upset because someone had said . . . and it is really hard to see your husband cry. And I said, "Honey, no matter what, we'll just go through this together." I was so scared (476-479).

And his friends said, 'You need to hurry up' and 'maybe you need to quit' and things like that. And Bob was just so scared, and I just said, "Honey, we'll get through this together no matter what it is, we'll get through it." And it was just, it's so hard to see your husband driving a car and crying, you know, and having to wipe his tears and . . . it was really hard (480-484).

For Bob and Kay, the loss of Bob's communication skills connected to every part of their life, including their financial well-being. Fear ran high because of the possibilities for enormous loss, which could occur if Bob lost his livelihood as radio manager.

Family Two: Clay and Pam discuss fears

Pam talked about being afraid and how frightening it was to consider the survival of their family dreams, relationships, and her husband's health:

I would say all the way along from day one, it was just very scary to be told 'Well, your husband is going to have

CHAPTER SIX   JOYCE

trouble talking for the rest so his life.' With no explanation, you know, 'Okay, he had a stroke, it hit this area of his brain,' and that's it [Laughing] (619-622).

That was another scary situation. Well, how were we going to survive? We still had young children and had college in front of us for them. And how was this going to affect us as a family being able to meet the goals that we had set? That is basically why he decided to go into the consulting business so he did have an income, even though, he did retire and selling the business, of course, that was an income. I also at that point decided that I needed to get involved in something as well and started talking to the National Aphasia Association about working for them (539-546).

We were pretty much on eggshells for a long time, and finally, I guess after the first six months, and he really wasn't doing much better with his speech (483-485).

He went back on the coumadin and I said to the doctor, "We will never, never go off of this again.' And he was on coumadin when he had the aneurysm rupture. So of course, we changed doctors. And the new doctor agreed that he should stay on coumadin and they again at that time put him through all these tests again; and again found nothing. But I just said, "Just for both of our mental and emotional well being he needs to stay on coumadin" (268-273).

Finally, he realized he wasn't worried about or dealing with stroke. He was dealing with aphasia. He had to live with aphasia for the rest of his life (630-632).

Also, our relationship changed because he was scared, and I was scared (479).

And she was just not embarrassed about her dad, but she wasn't, I could see a change where she was scared for him and she really, she would show her affection and then stand back. It was like, what is happening to my dad? Why can't he talk? She really was having a hard time understanding what had happened to him (302-306).

Pam and Clay's fears were for his mortality, health, career, their children's futures, and their relationship. For this couple, as for Bob and Kay, fear gripped each part of the security they had previously known. With none of the other associated stroke problems, in this case, the language memory loss disorder was the main reason for fear if indeed Clay survived to be the family provider, which he did not. In fact, his mortality was his biggest concern. However, he did live for five years and had already conquered the language memory loss completely during the last three of them.

Family Three: Eve and Sarah discuss fears

Eve and Sarah were the only participants who were living through the critical acute phase of the stroke and serious global language memory losses with many unanswered questions. Eve's fears of her mother dying were a part of her life and discussion during the interview:

CHAPTER SIX   J O Y C E

I can leave her home for a couple of hours, you know, go to lunch, because I've learned like you know for her to use the phone and all, but I still always worry that God forbid there is a fire, you know, or something. Is she going to be able to call me? Is she going to have to get out? Am I going to get home on time? Even if she gets the little button, I feel, kind of you know, kind of the call button. But still I always worry. I never go out with peace or a clear head. I always worry unless there is somebody here to watch her (493-499).

Because my mother's life could be taken away in one second . . . I don't really feel like anything is important anymore except for my mother to get better . . . (515-519).

If my mother was to pass away, it would probably take me a while to get over the guilt and all the other things that came along just for her going through this and maybe I didn't do this exactly the way I should have. You know, you put guilt on yourself. I probably would maybe go back to the way things were. Maybe a little bit better because I've experienced how life can be taken away so quickly (539-544).

    Eve had great difficulty dealing with all the elements of fear that her mother's precarious health posed for her future. The prospect of her mother's death became one of her imminent fears as well. Though she expressed early on in the transcript that 'mom was no longer mom' while she could not communicate with her and cared for her, nonetheless, the fear of her mother's death loomed largest in Eve's mind.

Family Four: Steve and Laura discuss fears

Well, isn't this incredibly encouraging to see: No fears remained for this couple or their family 14 years after language memory loss from stroke. These problems do find an ending!

Reflections on fears

At the time of the interview, the long-term cases of Steve and Laura, Bob and Kay, and Clay and Pam had already passed through the point of fear to the place of actual realization of fears and on to the state of losses mentioned in other categories. Fear for them was recalled as a piece out of the past that departed by the time of the interview, though loss was an ongoing reality. For the acute case of Sarah and Eve, the fears of what might happen were still alive and well. For Steve and Laura, after fourteen years, fear was no longer a major part of their life. They had survived very well and had quite a victory story in actual fact. Instead, a common theme in their story was concern for others that might also pass through their ordeal.

CHAPTER SIX   JOYCE

> *Subchapter VI-6. Family living arrangements, adjustments, situations, and behaviors of children.*

    Overall changes in the behavior of children and in the families' typical configurations occurred in many instances, but most often when the children still lived in the home. Family configuration changes seemed to be a part of this event for a variety of reasons. Language memory loss and its consequences appeared to bring on normal life cycle changes somewhat prematurely for older children still in the home where the memory loss person resided. Indeed, with no stroke the scenario of rearranged living conditions would be less likely to occur. The usual implication of neurological language memory loss was that life style changes occurred for most family members who lived in the household. The manifestation of change depended upon the family setup. In addition, behaviors of the children, such as acting out or serious emotional displays became more common during these events.

Family One: Kay and Bob discuss family living arrangements, adjustments, situations, and behaviors of children.

    For Kay and Bob, she described the changes that occurred with the older children that began to take place as each one moved out, except for the youngest child, during the event. She also spoke of how the children reacted emotionally to their father's language memory loss impairment:

DON'T FORGET

Karen moved out right after the stroke . . . Karen ended up moving out and going to live with somebody else (898-899).

Karen moved out after the stroke. So you see, I don't think she could bear to see her dad, I think that was really hard on her (918-919).

I think Joanie was probably a little more realistic than the other ones, but they weren't around him as much as Joanie. Joanie was the youngest one (767-768).

Well, she was talking suicide and I remember she said some things that she was doing. She had always been a little bit that way (818-819).

And then, Bobby was going through some rebellion and things, and then, in his junior year, he just up and told us in the middle of the year that he was going to go live with his mom, and she was going to buy him a car, and she did. He wrecked it on the highway within months and got the Stevens' girl pregnant afterwards and got kicked out of school (924-928).

Bobby wasn't bathing or shaving. I think he was in incredible depression, now that I look back (932-933).

He (Bobby) got kicked out of school in late September (976).

CHAPTER SIX   JOYCE

And Peggy just totally locked me out of her life. She would come and she would come home. And I think when she was home for one summer, she felt like I hadn't told her everything about her father. And I would write to her every weekend and call her in the middle of the week. And I didn't know what else to do but she still accused me the next time of not telling her everything (952-956).

So I would write to her in as much detail as I thought of and . . . so she was mad at me (962-963).

She wouldn't pay her car payments and oh, it was terrible. She ended up turning in her car, which was a leased car, and they slapped us with a $6,000.00 bill (899-900).

Karen had moved out and she didn't communicate with me at all (1017-1018).

Like when Karen's car, when Karen wouldn't pay for her car (1041-1042).

Peggy would come home all summer like I told you, she would speak ten words to me, have two meals with us or eat pizza in her bedroom (1019-1020).

This talk from Kay revealed that although she clearly knew from a factual perspective what had happened in her family since Bob's neurological memory and word loss, she had not connected all of the possible consequences with the children to her husband's language losses. Instead, she often saw the entire period of life as holding many unrelated spontaneous occurrences. She correctly viewed young adulthood as a stage, which can create inherent difficulties regardless of other circumstances. In negotiating meanings and outcomes from Kay's perspective, it can only be ascertained that Bob's stroke and memory loss played a strong factor, but cannot be viewed as the only one.

Family Two: Clay and Pam discuss Family living arrangements, adjustments, situations, and behaviors of children.

Pam spoke of the children and how they originally reacted to the changes. With time they began helping with their father's speech needs:

She was becoming a teenager and starting to have boyfriends or thoughts about boys on her own, which I think girls at that time start looking at their father like 'is this the type of person I want,' and of course she idolized her dad. So it was, and she was doing a lot of comparing, doing a lot of comparison in relationships of her own. And also, you know, girls, I think, go through this thing about their dad about don't touch me, don't kiss me in public [Laughing]. So she was also trying to deal with all that. Anyway they worked through all that and they had a very close relationship. I don't feel like it fell apart. It was just that some distance set in. I think that distance first concern certainly set in. She was concerned that he wouldn't live from the stroke at all (345-359).

CHAPTER SIX   **JOYCE**

When it first happened, though, she would not invite any of her friends over to the house. It was almost like she was embarrassed about it all. And we all understood that and we dealt with it and she realized it down the road, and she talked about it later and said that she just really was scared that her dad was not going to get better (310-314).

So, I guess in the beginning, the first several months, it was hard for the kids, even the younger ones, to realize that their father could not talk to them the way he used to and make the decisions about what they were going to do, or discipline them for something they had done and that they had to come to me (384-389).

The girls, well, the five year old, was learning how to read in kindergarten. And of course the four-year old was right behind, and she was interested in that, too. And they would read their books to Clay (291-293).

And then, Clay would try to read the sentences back or the word. This wasn't right away, but later, down the road, and it really became like part of his homework. It was fine with them because they were helping daddy to get better, and so they really enjoyed that. Now my teenager, who was in high school, or beginning high school at the time, she, I think, had a harder time dealing with it emotionally. At that time, you're very, you're just going through a lot of changes in yourself and your parents are there, but you, a lot of kids think that they know more than their parents at that age. [302-306. See *Fear*, p.133] I tried to give her the literature from the Aphasia Association to read, but it was almost like she put a block up about it, and just wanted it all to be gone, and for him to be normal again. As he started getting better over the years, she relaxed totally and their relationship was always a good relationship but it became very strong again (295-310).

The kids they really did join all together in helping in one way or another. Now when my oldest daughter realized that he was getting better then she too joined in, in helping with his homework, because he did have homework from this therapist every time he met with her, and we would all help with that. She became very active in her role, too, as a teenager, helping him out (314-318).

And he could drive again . . . my teenager enjoyed doing that with him and testing him to make sure he could read the signs (323-326).

Pam and Clay showed that the tough consequences for small children would be those down the road. The other life style changes due could easily be incorporated into their young lives and Pam made no mention of any serious difficulties for the younger children. If anything, Clay's young children enjoyed assisting their father and became involved in his recovery process. As it was for Kay and Bob's family, the older teenaged child in Clay's family experienced the more severe impact during her father's recovery and before his death six years later. However, the younger children would eventually suffer as well for loss of their beloved father. Had Clay survived, though his small children experienced some frustrations in the beginning of his disorder, the affects on them can only be surmised as minor. This is based upon the improvements he made to his language abilities such that Pam reported a complete recovery three years post-stroke onset and that the children enjoyed helping him make those improvements.

Family Three: Eve and Sarah discuss family living arrangements, adjustments, situations, and behaviors of children.

Eve's children were also teenaged and older when the stroke brought their grandmother into their home rearranging the setup of their nuclear family. Eve's experience of this disruption within her family placed her in a very difficult position:

I had left my house. My daughter was here to watch my mother that night. I was supposed to go over and do ceramics, what I usually do and I walked out and my daughter kind of just also gave me the news that she was moving out of the house. And I used her for helping me with my mother. So now I was like completely being abandoned with this disabled person. I just lost total control, screaming, ranting, and raging. I mean, you know I don't know what I'd done. I might have even hurt myself that night (287-293).

But he sleeps in the next adjoining room to hers. And he is a sound sleeper, but in the mornings when she wants to get up and dress and change and we don't come right into her room, she starts carrying on and she wakes him up . . .

DON'T FORGET

I know through my middle daughter, he made a comment to her that he can't wait to go away to college next year to escape this. And I guess it's his grandmother, it's hard for him to accept her being the way she is. But he is very good with her (86-93).

And then all of the sudden, she couldn't even tell me. She had her older sister tell me she was moving out. Because for my mother to move in, my daughter gave up her bedroom and she was going to share a room with her brother . . . They were just going to sleep in the same room. Basically, they lived different lives, but they were just going to sleep there. This way, I had a room for my mother to come home to. So she decided she didn't want to share a room with her brother. Meanwhile, she never really got to share a room with him because he was away for the whole summer. So she never got to do it (325-334).

She always said she couldn't move out for a long time because she had all these bills to pay. And . . . I adjusted. I got used to it. She still comes by once in awhile. Like I said, I don't leave my mother, but she'll come by like on Saturdays if I'm gone for the afternoon to go to ceramics, she'll come by and make my mother her lunch or just check up on her . . . And everybody was abandoning me with this condition and I didn't know where to turn for outside help (321-349).

Eve had made a promise to her mother not to abandon her to a nursing home, but later began to

CHAPTER SIX   **JOYCE**

experience difficulty in keeping her nuclear family stable while caring for her mom as the children began to change their living arrangements. The stress for Eve because of the numerous life style changes required in her case added to her pressures of having a language memory loss parent to care for.

Family Four: Steve and Laura discuss family living arrangements, adjustments, situations, and behaviors of children.

Steve and Laura added only a short reflection on the grown children and their ongoing concern. One of the children relocated and moved nearby to be closer. There were no live in children.

Reflections on family living arrangements, adjustments, situations, and behaviors of children

Participants in my study were aware of what had happened in their lives since the lost memory. Some saw connections between the language memory loss and the children's actions and changes in living arrangements, especially their older children. Since adolescence and young adulthood hold their own concerns, the confusion of mixing the problems of that life cycle with the occurrences of the memory loss patients, which are more typical in later life cycle stages, appeared to create a clash of emotional upheaval within the families. Though this produced discomfort, not all difficulties were for naught and some even seemed to increase the maturity levels of the children who joined in to help the patient regain communication skills. However, some families experienced the severity of being in untenable situations regarding living arrangements. Problems with children in language memory loss families typically occurred only when the children were also living in the home that the person inhabited and returned to after the stroke. The 14-year couple with adult children did not experience changes with their children other than increased concern and support and one son moving closer to their home. On occasion, they felt very gratified by the assistance of their daughters-in-law.

CHAPTER SIX   **JOYCE**

> ➢ **Subchapters VI-7. Role reversals and changes affecting family dynamics**

All families shared numerous changes to their families' systems and ways of functioning that occurred in relation to the loss of communication skills in the person with memory loss such that role reversals resulted. The reversals are discussed here:

Family One: Kay and Bob discuss role reversals and changes affecting family dynamics

Kay explained what occurred in Bob's parenting because of the change in his mental and communicated abilities.

Well I think he would have come across a lot stronger, in who he was as their father (597-598).

And especially one that was really acting up, and Bob couldn't handle him. And I was the step-mom and I couldn't handle him. And um, I just felt like I was totally worn out (563-564).

Yeah, because, you know what, he used to be the one that stayed up and made sure the kids got in, and now he was tired (601-602).

With Joanie, I know we would sit down and talk with her sometimes. And we would talk to her about what we were going to say, and I would say it. I think it would have been better if he had been able to say it, because my husband was a master with handling people. Not just because he knew how to communicate, I mean because he could talk, but because he knew how to communicate (1127-1132).

And but I think that when Bob lost that ability to reason without using words, loss of so many words. You know, it had to be me that did the reasoning, even though we would talk about things, you know (1142-1144).

One area or Kay's life that began to surface and overlap into other categories related to the issue of her step-parenting Bob's children. With or without language memory loss, step-parenting was Kay's only parenting experience. This issue became more imminent and more of a concern for her because of her husband's poor memory for effective communication that occurred between himself and his teenaged and older children.

Family Two: Clay and Pam discuss role reversals and changes affecting family dynamics

Pam described how her role as parent changed because of Clay's language memory loss:

Then once we got home and got into a routine, and I think the first few months were very difficult, because he could not say anything that made any sense, and I think she was embarrassed and it started changing their relationship where everything came to me (361-364).

CHAPTER SIX   **JOYCE**

Where I was doing all the decision-making, all the disciplining because, Clay couldn't. So the roles changed there tremendously. Before we had done it together and now it was all me, and it was very hard for him, too, because he had felt he had lost his role as a parent (364-367).

Well, all of them, as time went on, and even at that beginning point, Tara, the oldest, and Mimi, the middle child, had homework to do, and Clay and I ran our household totally together. It was 50-50 and we helped with everything together. So he would help with homework as well as anything else going on. So all of that switch over to me, as well as, just running the daily financial part of running a house. We did it together but than it all became my responsibility because of him not being able to work with numbers, that type of thing (376-382).

So, I guess in the beginning, the first several months, it was hard for the kids, even the younger ones, to realize that their father could not talk to them the way he used to and make the decisions about what they were going to do, or discipline them for something they had done and that they had to come to me. And I was trying to include him, you know, as much as possible, but after a few weeks the girls realized that they weren't going to get a response from dad so they had to go to mom anyway. So they cut him out. It was very hard to try and explain to them that we had to discuss this with daddy and he had to be in on the decision even if he couldn't talk to us, we had to

DON'T FORGET

discuss this as a family . . . (384-392).

But the roles definitely switched and the girls, you know, I think had a hard time accepting that daddy wasn't there as much as he was before . . . (398-400).

Our roles as husband and wife changed. Because even though we shared a lot of the responsibilities of raising the kids. He could not discipline. He could not help with homework. So all of that became my responsibility. Then the kids like I said before would come to me for everything (473-477).

For Clay and Pam, their big change with the children occurred in the parenting roles when he was 'cut out' of the decision making because of his communication. Pam felt the pressure of carrying the parenting role alone when Clay was no longer able to respond to the girls, discipline them, make decisions, or help with homework as he had done in the past. This was a "tremendous" change to their previous method of helping one another as they had always observed an unspoken "50-50" work division in the past.

Family Three: Eve and Sarah discuss role reversals and changes affecting family dynamics

Eve discussed her detachment from her mother brought on by the role reversal imparted by language memory loss and stroke:

CHAPTER SIX   **JOYCE**

Now, I'm feeling I'm becoming detached from my mother. I don't, I don't see her as my mother anymore . . . So I just look at her and see a responsibility right now. Something that I took on to take care of her because I love her so dearly, something I promised her that if she ever had a stroke I would do, I would take her home and take care of her. And that's what I'm doing . . . I feel more I'm the mother and she's the child (166-184).

She only wants me to do for her and that is it. And I think my mother also believes that she is not that tough to do, it's not a lot of work [when it is] (363-364).

But since she's been home to my house my sister hasn't called at all. She's like disconnected from the family. My brother is a good son and good brother; however, as long as he calls and I tell him everything is wonderful, that's fine. As soon as I give him any complaints, like if he calls me on a really depressed day, and I'm having a rough time, he doesn't want to hear it. His answer to me is, "Put her in a nursing home and if you don't, I don't want to hear your complaints anymore." So like I don't even have that. I have like nobody to unload on. And I should have my brother (452-459).

Well, I'm definitely a caregiver, without a doubt. I mean never in my wildest dreams did I ever think that I would be changing my mother's diaper, or having to give my mother a shower, or watch every little part of her body and make sure nothing is breaking out or anything. I never thought that this would ever happen (553-556).

DON'T FORGET

Eve experienced a severe role reversal that upset her a great deal in regard to her global aphasic mother. Her mother was no longer the mother with whom she was familiar and her new role had unbalanced her own family where she also carried the role of parent. As an adult child, Eve was now burdened with her mother becoming more like another child to her and with herself being child to no one. According to her remarks, her loss and the changes affected her dramatically.

Family Four: Steve and Laura discuss role reversals and changes affecting family dynamics

Laura had more to say about changes that affected reversals in Steve's personality than Steve did. She also discussed role changes from becoming a caregiver. Their remarks showed some occasional tension occurred between them in being a caregiver and person with memory loss affecting language:

Laura: Mr. Crank. He was so good before. You know anything, "Oh sure, here, have it." But afterwards and everything I do is wrong (262-263).

Laura: And you can document this, the care-giver always dies first (347).

Laura: I worked so hard to get my husband to the point he was at . . . (680).

CHAPTER SIX   **JOYCE**

I: The aphasia, could you tell me about it?
Laura: I don't know if he can remember.
I: He just said . . .
Steve: You know Laura, you don't let me ever talk.
Laura: I do let you talk. Okay. What do you remember?
Steve: I remember that I couldn't speak (83-88).

For a long time, Steve's memory loss placed Laura in a position to assist him. She had become his expert in communicating. This added qualities of a parent-child relationship. Steve continued to be somewhat one-down to Laura in communicating effectively. This represented a role reversal. This was not obvious to a casual observer because in every respect, they were a well-matched loving couple.

Reflections on role reversals and changes affecting family dynamics

Naturally, parents raising children experienced role reversals in dealing with children. Spouses took over the parenting role either permanently or until the neurologically impaired person experienced some recovery. Where the children were raised and out of the home, this was less pronounced. However, when a grown child became caretaker to a parent, Sarah and Eve experienced the most complete role reversal to their parent/child roles. Even though Eve's parenting of her own children was still intact, her mother became like a child to her. This lack of support from the mother she knew and grieved losing was painful and hurt her ability to go on in her other roles while care-giving.

DON'T FORGET

> *Subchapter VI-8. Marriage relationship losses*

Marriage relationships also changed after one spouse became neurologically impaired and became unable to communicate. Also, when a married child cared for a parent who had no partner to do so, there were marital changes within the caregiver's marriage. Each of the participants gave their views and had uniquely different situations in this regard.

Family One: Kay and Bob discuss marriage relationship losses

Kay's loss of a romantic partner was keenly felt as she expressed the metamorphosis that their relationship endured prior to Bob's death six years after the stroke:

But you know one nice thing that happened was before Bob had the strokes, I was his cheerleader. I was his encourager. And after the strokes, he was my cheerleader. Now it wasn't an instant change, you know. But it was like, when he died, I lost my faithful supporter. I wasn't exactly romantic about someone who was more like a grandfather than a father or even a husband (514-519).

You know it was like I really married an elderly gentleman. But the one thing that was neat about it was he was my staunch supporter. He was living for my dreams now instead of me living for his dreams (521-523).

CHAPTER SIX   **JOYCE**

And um, I just felt like I was totally worn out. And it was just a really . . . I don't know when it happened, I don't know when it happened. I knew I still loved him, but there was something missing. And he just wasn't my hero anymore. But he was my very dear friend (564-567).

I had changed in my relationship with my husband and it distressed me a great deal (550-551).

And then all of a sudden I had to be the hero for myself. And I didn't like that role and it was just so hard (513-514).

I never stopped thinking that he was going to go back to being my hero again. I never stopped (1013-1014).

And we had the first part and the second part of our marriage. But I felt like I was always married to two men. I felt like I called them first Bob and second Bob. I never said good-bye to first Bob until he died and then I had to bury two husbands almost (524-527).

His voice was only part of it. I mean it was who he was that was so good and then he lost that. And then all of a sudden I had to be the hero for myself. And I didn't like that role and it was just so hard (512-514).

And you know I always felt like a little girl all my life even growing up. I was always the beautiful bride of Bob Smith. I'm, not that I'm beautiful, but that's how I felt. You know I felt like the young, pretty bride of Bob Smith. So you know, I always had that nice feeling of being

DON'T FORGET

somebody that was a little bit unusual and different (554-558).

I felt very loved. I felt very attractive. I felt so much I just didn't feel old, but after he was in the hospital and I was carrying all those burdens around with me, the burden of still having children in the house (560-562).

I think it was okay if he made a mistake in front of me, cause sometimes we would laugh about it (1106-1107).

There were many changes in the meanings and roles in life that had significant impact upon what Kay believed to be the earthly end of her relationship with Bob upon his death. Kay effectively used metaphors spoken to her by a counselor/minister in expressing these changes in her interview. Kay also was very successful in accepting the changes in her marriage because of the disorder and found ways to love Bob differently, but just as much as before.

Family Two: Pam and Clay discuss marriage relationship losses

Similarly, Pam described the marriage relationships twists and turns:

Also, our relationship changed because he was scared and I was scared. As far as the sexuality part of it, our relationship was very good before and now it was, 'If we had sex is he going to have a heart attack? Is he going to have another stroke?' There were so many questions because they didn't know why this had happened to him. We were pretty much on eggshells for a long time, and finally, I guess after the first six months, and he really wasn't doing much better with his speech. He was feeling better and getting stronger. We relaxed and realized okay this was not something we were going to click our fingers and this is all going to go way and get better . . . This is long term and we are going to have to deal with and we need to go on with our lives and be a family again (479-490).

And he is going to be able to go back to work even if it is a little bit. And he is going to be able to go out in public and be with his friends again and play golf and do things that he likes to do, and things that we can do. And our relationship went back to the way it was before with me having to help a little more than I did in the past, but not tremendously (494-498).

So then, the roles started going back little by little and our relationship went back to I felt more secure that, 'No, he's not going to die tomorrow or the next hour or whatever (492-494).'

Prior to Clay's death, Pam expressed that the marital relationship did return to the way it had been prior to stroke. Clay earned his family's respect and strengthened his marital bond by working to improve. The wife and family also earned Clay's respect and love as they did all they could to help him return to his pre-aphasia state. Though Clay died, this family worked to live with the problems and re-align their marital and family relationships as well as they could in consideration of the various family dynamics.

Family Three: Eve and Sarah discuss marriage relationship losses

Eve discussed her relationship with her husband, son-in-law to her ill mother:

Well, he works seven days a week like almost 24 hours a day, but he's here to sleep . . . Yeah, he had a lot of work, a lot of jobs . . . Actually, there's just a little more tension on my part. Like I argue more with him because I'm more stressed out . . . He works . . . Well he goes to work at 6:30 in the morning and he gets home at 3:30; and he goes back to do another job at 5:30 until about 10:30 . . . . He's gone a lot . . . and I don't argue that much, but considering (102-119).

Eve revealed the marital situation between she and her husband as stable, yet, plagued with the stresses of life. Her husband's decision to remain at work a great deal appeared no different to her than in the past, prior to his mother-in-law's language memory loss. However, in negotiating outcomes at the second meeting, Eve admitted to me that her husband did occasionally speak of feeling a little like a "boarder" in his own home when discussing the facts surrounding Eve's mother living in the home.

CHAPTER SIX   **JOYCE**

Family Four: Steve and Laura discuss marriage relationship losses

Laura handled Steve's memory loss difficulties effectively, as he did, over many years. Their marriage was strong from the start of the crisis and revealed the ability to adjust and maneuver through the stages of Steve's ailments as they occurred:

Laura: The surgeon was very firm. In fact, they were concerned when he was in the intensive care. And he would invite me into the doctor's lounge and he would talk to me and tell me that I'm 53 and I should go on with my life and put my husband in a nursing home. But I said to him, on more than one occasion, "I could never do that, I'll bring my husband home, and I will take care of him." And he was trying to make me understand that I couldn't. Every once in a while when he really gets me angry I say, "Oh, I should have listened to Dr. N" [all laugh]. Once he really believed me after awhile that I was going to take my husband home, and I would not allow him to be in a nursing home he said, "Alright then, he'll start therapy" (365-373).

Wow! What Laura just said is so important. What a shift the doctor made when he saw the wife's commitment! In systemic family therapy circles, we speak of "the difference that makes a difference" (Bateson, 1972, p. 318). In Steve's case, Laura's response to her doctor was the difference that made the difference for both of them and for the future direction of their lives and the healing of the disorder. The strength of their commitment and marital bond promoted healing as the only alternative. Clearly, many families in this day and age do not realize the implications and ramifications of their responses to health care professionals, and how very important they are in determining how their future will play out. Physicians can not usually announce to family members that their determination and motivation will possibly be the deciding factor to the physician as he or she decides how the case will proceed and whether to provide rehabilitation and care for the future of the stroke victim their loved one or not.

Despite the choice Laura made to take care of Steve at home, this marriage relationship did change and adapt as a result of the 14-year long-standing language memory loss and stroke disorder. Throughout their interview, Steve commented gratuitously to Laura if she happened to correct his language memory. He appeared to accept her corrections as attempts to assist him. This seemed to work well for them and for the most part, Steve appeared to be accustomed to Laura's efforts. However, the chronic nature of language memory loss did create changes that would not have been in the relationship prior to memory loss when Steve was an excellent speaker. Nonetheless, this couple was evidently bonded such that they were able to handle this difficult life cycle transition with grace and dignity.

Reflections on marriage relationship losses

Language memory loss disorders appeared to affect the marriages in my study most significantly when ongoing spousal care-taking and role reversals occurred and went on well beyond the acute stage into the chronic phase of the disorder. Similarly, in those cases where the spouse took on a teaching role with the patient, there were changes in the marriage. This did not mean a spouse should not assume the role of caregiver or teacher as needed. However, attention to one's marital relationship would require one to attend to this on a day by day basis judging the value of continuing in the role if it was not typical to that marriage or if the personalities of the persons involved prohibited it. If such a role continued to have value and merit that the neurologically impaired person desired, then there would be no reason to cease care-giving or teaching behaviors handled judiciously and not given in a spirit of one ups-man-ship. Cessation of these behaviors when or if they become problematic could best be deciphered in systemic family therapy or in joint speech therapy/family therapy consultations.

DON'T FORGET

> *Subchapter VI-9. Life style losses—Personality, social, financial, and career related*

Each family had numerous other losses beyond the basic speaking, language or marital difficulties. During their discussions, they often spoke about personality and life-style changes that occurred due to the disorder requiring adjustment:

Family One: Kay and Bob discuss life style losses—Personality, social, financial, and career-related.

Kay described losses for Bob attributed to his vocal language memory change:

He used to work at the church and he used to laugh and tease them and everything. Then after his stroke, they complained to Lilly [the assistant radio manager], because he would always kind of walk around them or if he saw them; he would go another way. And I think it was because he felt like he had to be something that he couldn't be to them. He just couldn't be who he was (1099-1103).

And I think that because he lost his voice he lost a lot of who he was to a lot of people. And he didn't. He felt like ashamed that he had lost it, not ashamed but upset that he had lost it; and didn't want to make a fool of himself (1103-1106).

CHAPTER SIX   **JOYCE**

And I heard people say, 'There's Bob Smith. Doesn't he look good? There's Bob Smith, oh!' I wished they would have walked up to him and shaken his hand, because I think he felt like he had to be somebody and he couldn't be that somebody anymore (1096-1099).

But then he couldn't handle taking care of this money deal. He just could think about how to do that. I was taking a lot . . . Doing a lot of stuff that he couldn't do anymore (1047-1048).

Well, I had to write the checks and the main responsibility . . . (1041).

He said, "Take it out," and then he looked at me and he said, "I'm going to take care of you." But he never did he couldn't . . . Even though he still earned the money, I had to start writing checks (577-582).

I don't know. I never thought he was going to die. I thought he was going to live to be old. Even though, it never even occurred to me (1033-1034).

The losses in the case of Kay and Bob were enormous and ranged across many areas of life including: work, broad changes in relationships, financial, social, occupational, personality changes and health.

Family Two: Pam and Clay discuss life style losses—personality, social, financial, and career-related.

Clay also experienced broad areas of personal and

lifestyle adjustment. Here Pam described losses specific to their business, his work, and their dreams for the future:

We were both ready and our relationship before the stroke was just very secure and very opened with raising the children as morally and with correct values, as we could. And trying to give them a lifestyle that they could appreciate and grow up in and become wonderful people (445-447).

It varied, depending on what he was doing, but at that point he was not going to work at all. We had turned the running of the company over to the vice-president. And he was at home and he did not go to work until the eighth month post stroke and then he only went three or four hours a day (199-202).

The only time that he would get into trouble was when he was in a situation that he wasn't familiar with or nervous about something. Then he would have trouble speaking. He did have trouble comprehending some of the bank issues with the company. And we decided to sell the business (216-220).

The stress was great from the business so we decided to sell the business. So this is now five years post-stroke, first stroke, and we decided to sell the business to reduce that stress for him. And we did that in February of '92 and May of '92, he was working as a consultant for the

CHAPTER SIX   JOYCE

company, but he only had to go in once a week and that was minimal (409-413).

[Clay's death] And he was out playing golf, by himself, and had the aneurysm rupture and of course, he didn't know what had happen to him. I got a call from the hospital that I needed to get up there immediately. And of course, I thought he had another stroke. But when I got to the hospital I knew when I saw him that it was not a stroke. It was something different and he only lived about another hour after I got there (418-423).

[Clay's death] It really was and it was a shock for the girls because I could not get a hold of them. They were all at sports or school activities and I could not get a hold of them. They did not get to see their dad before he died. Of course, the way we explained it to each other or tried to get through it, I guess was that it was best to remember him how we saw him that morning when he left; which he was happy and his usual self (426-431).

And then he had to . . . He did not have to take the driver's test over again, because he didn't drive for eight months, but then once he became confident again, we went down to the drivers' MVA, and they tested him just sort of off the record and said, "There was no problem," and he could drive again (319-323).

Then when he had the stroke a lot of things were questionable. Were we going to have to sell the business right away? Was he going to be able to go back to work ever? Was I going to have to take over the business?

DON'T FORGET

Which I did not know the in and out of running a furniture business, I knew I could learn it. I was a college graduate and I knew I could do it. I didn't want to automatically sell the business because I had hope that he would get better; and of course, he did too. This was his dream to own his own business, so we didn't just want to throw it away. So we worked very hard to find people to take over that for us for a hopefully a short period of time, and it did work out that way (461-469).

At that time, find somebody to check in on Clay and make sure he was okay, because he wasn't comprehending everything at the beginning [at work] (471-473).

I guess the biggest thing that had to be switched was probably having to do with the furniture company. We had planned to just keep building that and I think as time went on the stress from the running that many companies, that many stores, we realized that we couldn't build it as big as we had hoped to built it. And I had also once the children had grown, I had planned to join him with the running of the business, but we had wanted to wait until the children were all out of high school. So those plans did change (530-536).

Eventually, Pam and Clay experienced the ultimate loss when Clay died of a ruptured aneurysm. Originally, Pam feared that if Clay went off the medication to prevent blood clots, he might have another stroke. When he did, this second stroke added more weakness to his already precarious health. The frustration for Pam was that she had feared the physician's decision to take him off blood thinning medication and then when they accepted the doctor's decision, Clay did experience the second stroke. In other words, the fears she had for his health did become realities and eventually caused his actual loss of life by ruptured aneurysm. Clay needed blood thinning.

Family Three: Eve and Sarah discuss life style losses—personality, social, financial, and career related.

Still functioning at the acute stages of the disorder at the time of the interview, Eve had a great deal of difficulty and believed she had suffered great unrecoverable losses. However, with time, this would be subject to change:

Um, has been a whole change of our life. I had to give up everything. I feel very trapped in my house (9-11).

Basically, she stayed home a lot, just as she was getting older she got tired of doing things, but she was totally independent, she drove, and she would go to BINGO, and occasionally, you know, do her own shopping, her food shopping and just go to the clothing stores, you know, walk around the malls a little (122-123).

Well, I can't bring home an income of any sort and that brings more stress into our lives (145-146).

We were real close . . . And she was really a relative, I could say she was my best friend. You know I was real close to her. And even before I went through this depressed time, I would see her at least once a week, I'd go up to visit her. Cause even with the kid I babysat, I used to take him with me . . . We were real close . . . Now, I'm feeling I'm becoming detached from my mother. I don't, I don't see her as my mother anymore (151-167).

And my older daughter, which has my grandchildren, has three children, I don't do too much for her anymore; because I don't have the patience. And she gets angry at me often because I won't baby sit or watch her kids or things like that. I lost patience for my own grandchildren, which I used to have tons of patience for children in general. Because like I said that's what I did for a living. I babysat children (575-580).

Eve described intense loss due to both the memory disability, which took away her mother's connection with her, and the care-taking that accompanied the disorder in its setting as a by-product of stroke. Their closeness, their separate lives, her mother's independence, Eve's work, and Eve's other family relationships were all pieces of major life-changing loss that disrupted the stability of her life.

Family Four: Steve and Laura discuss life style losses—personality, social, financial, and career related.

Steve and Laura discussed the varied losses the language memory loss created in their lives:

CHAPTER SIX   JOYCE

Laura: His friends felt too scared to visit him (310).

Steve: Well, he just, what people do is once you have the stroke especially an aphasia stroke, they would rather turn their back and look away because it hurts them too much. I don't know. Maybe they're afraid it's catching. I don't know. You lose friends slowly, some right away, and some slowly (481-484).

When asked, how the memory loss affected them financially, they responded:
Laura: Terribly.
Steve: Well, I have no pension.
Laura: They sold the business. There were three partners and they found out after this happened to my husband.
Steve: They were afraid to run the factory, without me. I was vice-president of operations, I ran the factory that means not just the factory, from purchasing to shipping plus I did some sales myself, some foreign sales.
Laura: So it did hurt us
Steve: They thought that they couldn't run the business without me and before it fell apart they sold it (500-510).

Steve: Steve: Yeah, I was suicidal . . . And he [a psychiatrist] came up that well, I have that, you know, I lost so much, I lost my business, I lost everything, I couldn't fly, I had all kinds of problems.
Laura: So much for that psychiatrist!
Steve: You know that I was preparing for my retirement. I could do copper enamel. I could do pottery,
Laura: We did all kinds of artwork.

DON'T FORGET

Steve: We did everything. You name it we tried it.
I: You couldn't do that after.
Laura: He can't.
Steve: No, you need two hands.
Laura: And besides, he wasn't [able] his physical condition (648-669).

    Steve lost so much that at one point he became suicidal. Because Steve suffered loss in so many areas of his life, it was much harder for this couple to distinguish between the concepts of losses due mainly to the memory loss versus those due to the associated problems of stroke. Questions intended to stimulate discussion about communication often yielded conversations about the loss of self-help skills and other common physical disabilities such as the loss of use of his hands, arms, shoulders, and legs. However, here it is important to note that the loss of use of the writing hand results in another loss of communication, which is also often remedied in speech or occupational therapy. Although the loss of ability to use the writing hand resulted in a communicative loss, compensatory methods such as use of the computer were common solutions for Steve. Nonetheless, this physical disability affected Steve's ability to take a phone message, write a grocery list, or even jot down a number and is one more lost method of language functioning. Steve also incurred temporary loss of use of his swallowing muscles. This loss would also be considered as an associated deficit of stroke known as dysphagia (Appendix A, p. 226). Although this is a disturbance to swallowing, not speech or language, Steve also mentions it in discussing his aphasia because he worked on improving it in speech therapy. When there is dysphagia, mild dysarthria (loss of pronunciation) is often present as well. This was also true for Steve. His speech was somewhat labored. Since he worked so hard to recall the words, his work to regain language also assisted his articulation and swallowing. However, this is another example of the way in which other associated disorders of stroke can add confusion to discussions. Neurological impairment is at the root of each of the communication problems, even the writing problem, and neurological healing is similar across the board. Treatments may differ, but healing is similar.

Reflections on life style losses—Personality, social, financial, and career related

Typically, numerous other losses crossed into the many areas of family life as the memory loss language disability played itself out. The communication losses affected careers, self-help capabilities, finances, emotions, relationships, and other losses. Families also spoke of associated losses of stroke such as swallowing, and/or articulation (see Appendix A) and the losses of hand, arm, shoulder, or leg usage. Some of these were accompanied by ongoing physical pain and physical or occupational therapy appropriate to the injury.

DON'T FORGET

> *Subchapter VI-10. Outside and professional health care and psychotherapeutic support*

Participants continually referred to the professionals and others who assisted in the endeavors surrounding memory loss. These discussions were not limited to medical personnel.

Family One: Kay and Bob discuss outside and professional health care and psychotherapeutic support

Kay discussed the support system, which was available to her:

And the speech therapist, I didn't really talk to him except for that one time. And then when Bob was in rehab, I just went in and watched him. I didn't get a lot of support (730-732).

The first doctor was an Indian doctor from India, and I liked him so much. And he was very encouraging. And he never talked about anything happening. He just kept pushing us towards, let's work on this and work on this, but never saying . . . (688-691).

Then I had this other doctor and he said, "Well I don't really have a lot of hope about this things." And I thought I don't want to see you again and I never did (695-696).

Joanie was going through a rough time. And I went to take Joanie and I liked what the counselor was doing for

CHAPTER SIX JOYCE

Joanie, so I decided to share her therapy. [Laughing] And I did. But I don't think it was about Bob. I think it was more about Joanie (806-809).

And she [her counselor] said to me, "Kay, you just seem like such an old, beaten up, tired soldier" (553-554).

And um, I just felt like I was totally worn out (564).

I mean when Reverend Bose was in the hospital, he would say, "Kay, how are you doing?" And I felt like everybody was taking care of Bob and no one was taking care of me, and I'm falling apart (760-762).

And the minister told me, well he was a counselor. He said, "I don't think you're burying one husband. I think you're burying two." Because I never said goodbye,

I never gave up on my first husband. I just kept thinking, he could do it. He could do it. I think he knew that he could, but he didn't like trying (744-747).

And I know that is a very callous way to look at it, but I had nobody. I had the kids and they weren't facing reality anymore than I was (789-790).

Man, I wish I would have had family down here (775).

And it felt so good that I knew that I needed some support myself, at least with the step kids (845-846).

I waited for the doctor. Then one of the ministers came by

to give Bob something and he ended up talking to me all morning. And the doctor never came (666-667).

Support categories included all the professionals who dealt with Bob and Kay from the time of the stroke onset. All avenues of support were included, even those outside the health care profession. Bob and Kay's church assisted them regularly offering prayer and counsel. The minister/counselor there offered metaphors of value, which gave meaning to their serious dilemma. Indeed, these were strong in Kay's mind long after Bob had passed away and represent the interventions and territory open to family therapists in working with this disorder.

Family Two: Pam and Clay discuss outside and professional health care and psychotherapeutic support

Pam and Clay received medical support from their doctors, but still felt uninformed or supported until the speech therapist and the National Aphasia Association became part of their lives:

So they released him from the hospital after all these tests with medication for coumadin. It was coumadin that they gave him because they felt it had to be a blood clot that broke away from somewhere. They were guessing it was probably in the neck area, but they were guessing because they didn't really have any idea (125-128).

We were told when we got back to Maryland (pause) we did find a neurologist. That was simply, I wasn't given any direction in this at all. I simply looked up in the Yellow Pages. Then I talked to friends if they knew of any neurologist and at such a young age, there aren't too many people who have to see neurologist . . . So I just went with recommendations from people that I talked to and found a very good neurologist. The neurologist did hook me up with the speech therapist that we used who was excellent (172-176).

So you know at the time, he had his second stroke. Well six weeks before his second stroke, he went for a check up and the neurologist said, "You are doing great. There is no reason for you to be on coumadin. There is no indication that this will happen to you again. We can't figure out why it happened, so we're taking you off of coumadin." And I was with him at this doctor's appointment and I said, "Wait a minute, you know, I have read that the possibility of having more strokes is there, and you don't know why he had a stroke, and if you put him on a lower dosage of coumadin, wouldn't that be safer than just taking him off completely and taking that chance." And they disagreed and said that he was a young man and it shouldn't happen again. Six weeks later he had his second stroke, after he was taken off the coumadin. . . . I just decided that this was a fluke and they made a mistake and people make mistakes . . . He went back on the coumadin and I said to the doctor, "We will never, never go off of this again.' And he was on coumadin when he had the aneurysm rupture. So of course, we changed doctors (260-270).

Well, we did not know anything about support groups or

DON'T FORGET

what was available until we got involved with the National Aphasia Association (562-563).

So we came back to Maryland and talked to the speech therapist and asked, "Well, are there any? Where are they?" [Laughing] So thank goodness, there were two right in our area and they were called stroke support groups. But we called them and found out that they did have one group had two people who had aphasia and the other group had three or four that had aphasia. So we went to two support groups in different areas in our community. And it was interesting because each group was totally different. And, it gave us a good viewpoint from both sides and the ages varied tremendously, too, in the groups. We were probably the youngest until a young girl that was probably in her early 30's joined one of the groups. Really that was the only help for caregivers as well as for people with aphasia that we could find (582-592).

Well, one of the groups we went to and this was why we went to two different groups because one did not do this, but one of the groups had a meeting together and then they would break up into groups, the people with aphasia and the care-givers, and they would meet separately. They would attend to whatever topics were important at the time or a lot of times we had speaker come in, but they did separate into two different groups. Today, some groups are strictly caregiver groups and that is good, too. I found it. It was really important for Clay to be with other people who had aphasia to see that he was doing well, to

CHAPTER SIX   JOYCE

see where he had been, and where he had gotten to. And it was also very important for me to be with other spouses or other relatives that were having to go through the same emotional things. They had a lot of answers because they had been dealing with it for 20 years or whatever and they had a lot of suggestions. So it is very important to address those two groups separately, not all together every time. Some groups I know do meet together all the time and I've had many conversations with spouses in particular that they are just so frustrated because a lot of times they don't feel and I felt the same way, "I don't want to ask that question in front of Clay because I don't want to hurt his feelings or whatever." It is important to address both groups separately if possible (596-613).

In some areas, we do have community support groups throughout the United States. Some support groups do have a system with their hospital that they are contacted when a person comes in and has had a stroke and acquires aphasia, that they are allowed to come in if the family agrees and sit down with them before they are released, and give them some information about aphasia, but not every hospital has approved that (652-657).

Clay and Pam later sought the assistance of support groups after speech services became unavailable to them in their attempts to continue in Clay's journey to recovery and in hopes of finding needed answers from others like themselves. They found this support from groups to be meaningful and of utmost value to them. Again, in my own investigation of the stroke support and aphasia groups, I found the assistance of a family therapist to be a sought after commodity. Joint consultations should be part of the future.

Family Three: Eve and Sarah discuss outside and professional health care and psychotherapeutic support

Eve discussed her feelings about the support she received:

Maybe I'm looking for a lot more than they can give. I don't know. Considering I'm like one person never went through this before with anyone or heard about it from anyone. I don't know where to turn sometimes (272-274).

Eve: No. Very little support. In fact, even the social worker there in the facility she was in, I didn't really feel gave me that much support either. They didn't tell me too much.
I: What kind of support did they give you?
Eve: 'Good luck' (216-255).

I didn't really remember too much support. I mean, they gave me a couple of numbers to call like Home Bound, like people to get help in for her (257-258).

She [social worker] just advised me what I could do as far as regards to like I could get meals on wheels for her if I wanted. Cause I wanted to get originally on Medicaid and see what I could do for her otherwise. And also in case I needed a long-term facility, she needs to be on Medicaid. And at that point I was at my end. I couldn't do for her

CHAPTER SIX   JOYCE

anymore. This is, I guess, three months back or something like that, or two months back and she had told me how to go about putting her into a long term facility and getting Medicaid to pay for it. Even she didn't give me that much (264-271).

Oh, yeah. In fact, that social worker did tell me about that support group where I met you. She did tell me, actually, she didn't tell me, I asked her, 'Are there any groups?' And she referred me to that one . . . I was definitely at a crucial time. I don't know if I already had an emotional breakdown at that time or if I had it after. I think I must have had it prior to her coming (277-283).

He ordered it [rehabilitation therapies] again. He keeps on ordering it but it hasn't started. I'm supposed to give him a call this afternoon to see what's going on. . . . It comes in for every two [weeks]. The insurance company allows two weeks at a time so when it runs out he orders it again . . . So well then sometimes we have a lapse of a month in between and then they'll get started again (608-615).

I: So what do you think is going wrong with the ordering process?
Eve: I don't know. I think it's the insurance fault. I don't think it's the doctor. I think it's the insurance.
I: What does the doctor say it is?
Eve: I don't ask him, so I don't know.
I: He'll just say that he'll put the order in. Then he'll tell us, if you don't hear from them within a few days, call me again and he'll call it in again.
Eve: And some times when he comes he has to call in an

DON'T FORGET

order to get an order to go.
I: Twice
Eve: She saw her last Thursday I believe, and now it is already what? Today is Wednesday. It's almost a week away. I haven't heard from the occupational therapist or physical therapist yet.
I: So has he called it in twice now?
Eve: Well, I have to call him again and let him know that I haven't heard from them. I give them a few days, but like I said, today, I was going to call again (616-630).

They [the doctors] told me speech therapy [would help her]. But, then it was never ordered for her. She never got it. She came home to my house and it was only with me after talking to the doctor for a while, like two months down the road, she finally started speech therapy. Maybe a month and a half down the road. I don't remember exactly when, but it was a while (238-242).

I do. I do. But sometimes, she [her psychologist] tells me, 'Ah, I don't want to have to hear about all these things," cause it upsets her to see like you could have a stroke and just like that your life changes . . . We kind of have a friendship relationship. She's not really doing therapy on me right now. She just allowing me . . . She says, "I can't do therapy on you right now, because you have your problems." It's not like I manufacture problems that she can straighten out in my head. Well, see she can't correct my mothers' stroke. So she can't deal with that. She can't make that problem better . . . She definitely helps me (460-476).

CHAPTER SIX JOYCE

Eve's case revealed many sad occurrences in the professional health care support system. The ordering process for her mother's therapy was very difficult, so much so, that it appeared to her to be designed for frustration. In addition, her psychologist was unable to help her regarding the talk about stroke or the language memory loss The professional explained that these physical disabilities represented "real" problems, not one's simply in Eve's mind. Eve interpreted that she could only help with concerns that were psychological and therefore, these were inappropriate to a psychologist's intervention and support. These spoke to me of the need that these families have for therapists and support from those who have some understanding and are willing to intervene during these most critical life cycle circumstances.

Family Four: Steve and Laura discuss outside and professional health care and psychotherapeutic support

Steve and Laura believed the stroke support clubs were beneficial to their cause, but also had a disconcerting experience with psychology/psychiatry as described below:

Steve: You know why stroke club is so good? Because you can see what other people have overcome (356-357).

Steve: I'm going to tell you something about aphasia. When we were in the Rochester stroke club this guy Paul I knew had aphasia couldn't speak at all. And he came to

180

DON'T FORGET

the meetings all the time, we all spoke to him, and when I left Rochester he was talking (452-455).

I: You went to a psychologist once for an hour?

Steve: Yeah, I was suicidal . . .

I: How far into the stroke were you suicidal?

Steve: Right after I got out of the hospital I think. And anyhow, we went to the psychologist the doctor recommended him, you know, we don't know anybody. And I was, I couldn't fly a plane anymore, I couldn't drive, I couldn't do anything.

I: Sure, you're life was all different.

Steve: So anyhow, he agreed, I had reason to feel that way. He offered no help. And my wife and I, after one hour he interviewed me, he interviewed her, and he came up that well, I have that, you know, I lost so much, I lost my business, I lost everything, I couldn't fly, I had all kinds of problems.

Laura: So much for that psychiatrist! . . .

Steve: When he, Laura and I, when he decided I had reason to be suicidal

Laura: He spoke to each one of us separately and then he spoke to us together. And I wanted to kick the man out of the room. I mean I would have been on assault charges if I ever started. After speaking to me and hearing my whole story and then hearing my husband's story, he just sat there and I don't know what my husband said, to sit there and look at my husband and say, "Yes, Mr. K, you're right, I would want to commit suicide, too, if I were you." Would you not want to get up and hit him? I worked so hard to get my husband to the point he was at and he was with this Dr. S, and so he didn't know my husband also

had a brain tumor, I mean, so I signed him over to my Dr. H. I loved Dr. H. First thing she did when my husband came out of the hospital was put him into another hospital and they checked him, the reason he was so anemic he was losing blood. The tube had worn the esophagus. So anyway, I did everything I could to make him well. And oh, about 2-3 [years], right before we moved down here, we went to the psychiatrist. I thought, 'Well, maybe psychiatric help could do something for his speech." He sat there and said, "Well, I'd want to commit suicide too."
I: I'm telling you, what a response.
Laura: And we paid that man.
Steve: Well, you have doctors and you have doctors (642-691).

    Here, Steve explained that he told a psychiatrist he was becoming suicidal during his recovery. He and his wife went there for help, but the doctor's understanding of the recovery ordeal was again apparently limited. Therefore, the psychiatrist's lack of experience with the illness and his response to the dilemma compromised the only goals giving meaning to Steve and Laura's life at that time. Indeed, they expressed their belief that the psychiatrist's decision to agree with Steve's depression did not help them during his suicidal stage. In fact, Steve became more depressed and Laura felt that all her work to help Steve improve was challenged as worthless.

Reflections on outside and professional health care and psychotherapeutic support

For all practical purposes, the psychotherapeutic support

systems mentioned by the participants seemed the least adequate, and perhaps the most harmful, in some cases to the recovering persons and families. In the case of Clay, the speech therapist was noted to be the only provider of psychotherapy until they joined support groups. Pam continued to believe in speech therapy as their main form of support. Then there was Eve. What a sad account given about her psychotherapist, who said she could not help her with a real problem, only a psychological one! Need she be reminded, psychological problems are born out of real problems. Nonetheless, her unwitting remark reminds me that family therapists, who deal with real problems of more than one individual, are better equipped to assist both the family, the patient, the doctor, and the speech therapist when support is needed. Some psychotherapists also train with families. Some psychologists train in work with caregivers. In those cases, such therapists could be helpful. Ones who know something about neurological impairment would also be wonderful. Family therapy offers successful brief supportive models for real problems. However, the majority of family therapists and other psychotherapists would need to collaborate with the speech therapist if the goal is to continue working on the rehabilitation of language memory loss. That collaboration could assist families in targeting possible areas of successful entry for improvement.

So let's now discuss those who are the rehabilitation therapists. They are the speech pathologists (or speech therapists if you prefer that wording), who rightfully recognize themselves as the main ones offering emotional support, who can only do so much. Why? First, because they are paid to retrain the language memory loss and not enough funds are available even for that. Second, because they are not trained as psychotherapists. They are trained to consult the family, but only in respect to healing the memory disorder.

Many times the bewildered caregiver has no one and little hope when scant information is all that is given and when insurance provides so little. So people flounder because there is no other system of follow-up. There is no insurance coverage beyond some short rehabilitation, rarely enough, so why send out for emotional or coping support? Since speech therapists believe counseling comes with their territory, speech and language assistance is the one most mentioned and considered to be the supportive professional role from the health care profession for stroke memory loss (Uffen, 1998, p. 14). In the past this was true, but not enough under present conditions. Even what speech therapists know is not understood enough to be reflected in the diagnostic manuals written by those who never see these patients as much or as often. How can psychiatrists and psychotherapists possibly know the clinical moments? But what good is the truth about memory loss if documented diagnostic evidence is doled out with contrary information? If you have seen Helen Keller, you know the expert was the speech therapist/teacher who worked directly with her. Presently, family therapists and other therapists could be very helpful to caregivers. With the help of speech therapists, family therapists could offer consultations to assist families along with speech therapists to develop their own self-help methods long after speech training is over. Speech therapists could do the job alone if they are inclined to help families develop a plan for the long haul and for when they depart. Regular evaluations and visitations with the intent of ongoing maintenance and consultation to succeeding families would be joyfully embraced and welcomed.

In Kay's story, the counselor/minister offered helpful therapeutic intervention by using therapeutic metaphors to empower the narrative of Kay and provide meaning during the most difficult time of her life (Rolland, 1994). Certainly families should turn to anyone who has some level of compassion at a time like this. The process of recovery after any neurological damage is character forming and any sincere clergy or counsel will discuss that. Hopefully the psychologist represented in this study is not typical to the medical community in her responses. I am sure there are many therapists who would love to lend a supportive ear at a time like this. Nonetheless, I believe understanding the family system and the neurological problems leaves the major contributors for the future to the speech pathologist and family therapist.

Beyond that there is another frontier highly recommended in these family stories. There was a great response to support groups, both stroke and language memory loss groups from the National Stroke Association and from the National Aphasia Association. There are also numerous other illness specific support groups (Appendix C).

CHAPTER SIX   JOYCE

> *Subchapter VI-11. Coping and psychological manifestations*

The results of living with the memory loss problems and other related concerns led all of the participants to discuss the related emotional and psychological disturbances they experienced. Also, each of them had various ways they coped and dealt with the disturbing changes and emotional issues in their lives:

Family One: Kay and Bob discuss coping and psychological manifestations

Kay was very thorough in her interview and spoke about how the family coped with Bob's shift in communication and personality aside from receiving outside support. Kay was also able to report positive outcomes in Bob:

So they walked up to the room, too, and they prayed over him (64).

I was worried about the kids. I didn't think they were facing reality and I found out later of course that they weren't because they just thought their dad could still talk fine. And they weren't . . . I was thinking, wait a minute, where is you brain? I mean, you know, he's just fine, he's not just fine, you know (763-767).

They were really kind of in denial. I mean, they would say to me, after several years of Bob's speaking they would still say to me, "Well, Dad's okay" (150-151).

DON'T FORGET

You live in denial. That is the only way that you can handle that [Laughing]. That was why it was so hard when he died. And the minister told me, well he was a counselor, said, "I don't think you're burying one husband. I think you're burying two." Because I never said goodbye, I never gave up on my first husband (742-746).

I don't know because it was one of the most horrendous things that I ever went through. And I don't wish it on my worst friend (1154-1156).

And it hurt so bad, but once I wrote the letter and said goodbye to both of them, it started not hurting as bad (529-530).

Well anyway, so after he was sick he was so compassionate. He did not make heavy demands on me. Like that one time I told you, he put my teddy bear in my arms. That was something that would have never happened before his strokes (1185-1188).

Since the family was never given any expectations for improvement, Kay believed they moved into their positions of denial in order to function and develop acceptance in this place where they didn't know what might happen to Bob. She believed they denied the hard facts that his health could decline in favor of hoping for the best and accepting Bob's lowered communication abilities. This worked for the children with Bob as 'dad,' but was unacceptable to Bob and Kay in his work on the radio and in light of who he was to his wife in his pre-aphasia state. Kay began to speak more and more often of Bob as 'first Bob' and 'second Bob,' as though for her they were two different men, one the pre-aphasia Bob and one the post-aphasia Bob. She noticed that in his post-aphasia state, he became more compassionate. Also, their spirituality and Christian belief system continued as a method of coping and was always a part of Kay's ongoing story and their management of Bob's memory loss illness.

Family Two: Pam and Clay discuss coping and psychological manifestations

Pam described Clay's moments of frustration and acceptance and their mutual concern for his health that impacted them both in their emotional coping:

But he really didn't have any problems after the second stroke except depression. That hit very hard at that time and I think it was later he stated because when is this going to stop. Am I going to go through this every few years for the rest of my life? Why can't they tell me what's wrong with me (237-240)?

And he just worked very hard, but he did say that the aphasia was the hardest thing to deal with (513-514).

This is long term and we are going to have to deal with and we need to go on with our lives and be a family again (489-490).

[Medication] . . . [The doctor] put him through all these

tests again; and again found nothing. But I just said, "Just for both of our mental and emotional well being he needs to stay on coumadin" (272-273).

Clay experienced the common problem of depression, which so often sets in for memory loss patients. He continued to hold a desire that someone in the medical community would support him, give him some encouragement, or inform him about what the future might hold. Would he have more strokes? Would he ever really be better? The interesting point here is that though no one is ever sure what will happen, there is hope for almost complete improvement in people who continue to move in that direction with that goal in mind who are healthy enough to do so. Clay became one of those people without that encouragement from the medical community.

Family Three: Eve and Sarah discuss coping and psychological manifestations

Eve spoke from the perspective of a tired caregiver with her mother still working through the initial acute stage of global language memory loss. Eve's emotional distresses were visible as she discussed her methods of coping and the pressures in their lives at this time:

So it's gotten like easier down the road except that the same point emotionally, it's, I feel too trapped in my house. I can't escape. It's like having a child here. You can't leave a child home alone. So, you have to have a

CHAPTER SIX JOYCE

sitter or someone to take care. In my mom's case, she doesn't want anybody here other than me to take care of her. So it just left me a very trapped feeling. Psychologically, that's not really good for me (13-19).

This way I feel a little more relieved going out because she keeps on telling me "Go out, go out," that she's okay by herself, but that took a couple of months of being with her to see that she is capable of being home alone, and she's not a panicky type of person (54-57).

I was definitely at a crucial time. I don't know if I already had an emotional breakdown at that time or if I had it after . . . I just kind of like lost total control. I mean I went outside my house . . . My daughter kind of just also gave me the news that she was moving out of the house. And I used her for helping me with my mother. So now I was like completely being abandoned with this disabled person. I just lost total control, screaming, ranting, and raging. I mean, you know I don't know what I'd done. I might have even hurt myself that night . . . I mean I got to the point, I was just like, I, I was like just and I screamed in the neighborhood, "I'm never coming home again. You'll never see me again. I don't want to do this anymore. I can't handle it. You all have her now, I don't want to know about it." I'd just, I'd just never really lost the control that I lost, cause I'm always within control of myself. And only because I had the cell phone and luckily it had the therapist I see, the psychologist I see, I had the number on me in my car. Because my day planner that always has all that information, well, that was in the house, and I wasn't getting out the car to go in the house

DON'T FORGET

and get it cause I was like just too upset. And I called and they were even putting me into a hospital right then and there, because I was so bad. And I said to them, "I can't go into no hospital," cause I had my mother to take care of, you know? . . . [This was] after I took her home about two months of doing it [caring for mom] (281-316).

I look at life a little differently now . . . In that life can be taken away so quickly. And things that were important to me before are just not important anymore . . . Like even just how my house is done. Like if it's dirty, so it's dirty. Where before it would drive me nuts. So like it's not important. It's really not important. Or even just to have everything just perfectly matched. I mean I still like things to be that way, but it's just; the importance is just not that high anymore. It doesn't carry a lot of weight . . . Because my mother's life could be taken away in one second . . . I don't really feel like anything is important anymore except for my mother to get better . . . (504-519).

So she would never, never do anything that would harm me, so the fact that she is not accepting these women. I realize that it is completely out of her control (439-441).

Eve knew that her mother's sweet disposition had changed. Her personality suffered along with her brain when she was afflicted language memory loss. Knowing whom she had lost in her mother and that she could die instead of getting well continued to plague Eve as she attempted to cope with the new realities in her life and the

CHAPTER SIX　　　　　　　　　**JOYCE**

ongoing changes during the acute beginning stage of the condition. Indeed, Eve felt as if she was having an emotional breakdown from all the pressure when her own daughter, who helped her with her mother, moved out of the home. Coupled with that, her psychologist had framed the stroke and memory loss talk as something outside of her realm of expertise [460-476, p.179]. How disheartening! In fact, the results of my clinical experience and the conversations in this study tell me that so much of the needed work to be done for language memory loss and the families is very psychological. Any good psychotherapist should be able to help families plan and cope during aphasia language memory loss.

Instead, Eve's psychologist said she had become her friend, and also confessed she was no longer able to earn her pay by offering her support and bearing the burden of listening to her. That's when you say good-by to one therapist and hello to a new one! You shouldn't pay to talk to your friends. A therapist should be able to offer something different from everyone else or else why not go to your friends for therapy? Actually, a good start until you find a speech therapist who can perhaps collaborate with a family therapist to help you set up a family plan for recovery is anyone who can listen and care while you vent. Hopefully they won't shoot you in the foot like they did Steve and Laura in the next quotation!

Family Four: Steve and Laura discuss coping and psychological manifestations

Steve and Laura also expressed their

psychological concerns as frustrating. In the prior dialogue, [356-357; 452-455, p. 180] they relate their success in using stroke support systems. Steve expressed suicidal feelings after he came home from the hospital. Laura discussed her own feelings of shock as well. She also indicated her own difficult position as caregiver in explaining that caregiver spouses usually die before the ill spouses do.

Laura and Steve were realistic during his most difficult emotional stage of accepting his memory loss and stroke, even to the point of going for psychiatric help when he initially felt suicidal [642-691, p.181-182]. However, going to the psychiatrist did not offer them the solutions they needed. Laura continued to work hard as his caretaker, and eventually they did gain their support and coping strength through the stroke and aphasia support network. Steve and Laura overcame their difficult times and endured the disorder long-term.

Reflections on coping and psychological manifestations

Complete recovery may not be actualized or realized in patients with language memory losses even when attempts to improve are made; however, the opposite attitude of giving up and doing nothing appears more detrimental to these patients and their families. Indeed it appears that such a stance only adds to their downward turn. Coping does not appear to occur by sitting idly by with the belief that there is nothing to gain by trying to go on with life and be involved in the activities of daily living and speaking. Indeed the belief

CHAPTER SIX — JOYCE

that all is lost adds a dimension that appears to be hurtful to the entire family system. This is not to say physicians, family therapists, social workers, or rehabilitation therapists should offer any false hopes in serious cases, just some hope, founded on many real recoveries and, therefore, could prove to be helpful even if only small improvements result. This has been reconfirmed in all the discussions with my participants. Such an attitude reflects the true state of knowledge and education regarding the aftermath of living with ongoing language memory loss concerns. This also does not mean that one should push hope at the wrong time when a patient is on life support, unable to lift a finger, or sit up and take nourishment. Certainly, there will be understandable times and stages for allowing patients and families to feel hopeless as they count their losses and review their options. Even the psychiatrist was not totally off base in admitting that Clay had a rough time, but to say suicide is a good idea has never been an acceptable method of practice, nor was it sensitive to the wife as caregiver. It is okay that birds of fear fly over our heads now and then, just be sure not to let negative thoughts make a nest in your hair. Keep trying. Don't give up. That attitude is worse than living with the disorder in the case of language memory loss impairments. Eve and her mother would tell you. Steve would tell you. Laura would tell you. Pam, Kay, Clay, and Bob would all tell you. And they have.

DON'T FORGET

Chapter Seven

Amazing Stories—"To Do" and "Not To Do"

Much valuable guidance came from the long-term memory loss person, Steve, and also from his wife, Laura. He had outlived his memory loss by fourteen years, which is not unusual. Steve made the important point that after memory loss there are times of accelerated learning and other times when a plateau is reached, but plateaus do not last forever. There are learning spurts and waiting periods.

Let's review two head-injury stories with names changed to preserve anonymity. These stories reveal there are waiting periods, but over time, change comes. Persistence, patience, and endurance pay off in cases of memory loss. The following stories of Tina and Danny were personally shared with me and are jammed packed full of "how not to" and "how to" believe and behave when dealing with the growth spurts of memory loss.

Tina's Head Injury—
You Can't Believe Everything You Hear

This story proves: People begin to believe in and hold on to their disorders even when there is huge evidence to the contrary until a professional exonerates them. I have heard many similar stories to this one. I chose to share this story only because Tina asked me to let others know what happened to her to prevent her situation from happening to them.

Tina came to a support group describing her irreparable brain damage due to a head injury. She had been an elementary music teacher, proud of her career, who had remarried after a divorce. An unfortunate

CHAPTER SEVEN — JOYCE

accident occurred at her public school work place prior to the marriage, and over time she began to deteriorate and eventually became unable to function. The accident involved a heavy piece of equipment that fell and hit her on the head. During a four-year period, she began to have memory loss and other aphasia-like symptoms. She was forgetful and easily confused, plus her vocabulary and ability to focus and think began to shrink. She became unable to work, drive, organize, or do normal errands.

Many doctors tried to be helpful. Then one doctor told her the situation was hopeless, and she would continually decline for the rest of her life and end up in a nursing home. This was the last thing she needed to hear. Believing that doctor and based on her ill health and depression, she went to bed and told her new husband to leave her. After a year of that behavior, he did leave, encouraged to do so by two psychiatrists. Over the next six years, Tina says, all she did was sleep her life away.

Then she appeared at the support group and reported in a surprisingly animated and charming fashion how her life was ruined, and she was going to decline continually, growing progressively worse until her death. This was what she firmly believed. She and others at the group wondered if she should have surgery for her injury. I asked her if she was driving, and she reported that she had driven herself to our meeting place that day. Very quickly, it became obvious to me that she had either received bad information, or that over the years, it was unknown to her that she had very much improved.

Only after I pointed out to her that she was healing and not degenerating, did her life begin to make a complete turn around. You see, until another professional convinced her that she was getting better, she treated herself according to the hopeless prognosis and diagnosis: As a degenerating brain injured woman with memory loss and other aphasia symptoms, waiting to get progressively worse and worse until her death.

At first, she simply could not believe me when I told her she was getting better and went running back to see a neurologist. Both of them agreed she was doing fine. Tina was dumbfounded. Of course, this is exciting that she improved over the six years, but it is also sad that she sent her husband away and is now alone and he is with another woman. However, with a great deal of encouragement and therapy, she finally began teaching music again. Believe me, it took enormous courage for her to begin her previous work again. Sadly, this type of story is not uncommon to therapists. People are told they will or will not get better for many reasons: Liability, lack of certainty, or they simply avoid appointments for fear of more bad news. Others get better as Tina did and still believe they are sick, and act accordingly, because they are holding onto a hopeless prognosis or diagnosis.

A Neurologist's Examination

Have you ever gone into your doctor and then left without knowing one way or the other why you went in because you did not learn anything new? Tina continued going for evaluations with no hope inside herself. She went around letting others know her life was over because of her head injury, confusion, and memory loss. One can only imagine what happened at her various office visits.

Possibly Tina did not speak much, and therefore, the doctor may have missed her improvements. Maybe the doctor was busy or just quiet the day of her visit. The doctor's quietness may have made Tina more concerned.

CHAPTER SEVEN   JOYCE

Actually, it was meant to calm her and let her know she wasn't doing badly or he or she would have told her so. Maybe the doctor was frustrated and admitted not knowing what more could be done or why life was not back to normal for Tina. This sometimes only adds to the belief that the problem is severe when no one knows what else to do. A person can also become insulted when they are told they are fine after so much pain and suffering feeling the doctor does not respect or believe their story. After such an appointment, they become even more convinced of their illness to defend their position.

Essentially, after you hear any negative news about memory loss, remember to believe the best anyway because no one knows for sure whether healing will occur or not, and besides, the new evidence is now out. People do heal from brain damage even with counseling and psychotherapies (Rossi, 2002). Furthermore, you cannot get to the healing place while holding onto the grim reports and deep-seated negative beliefs and suggestions to the contrary. Personally, I tend in many cases not to read the case reports from other therapists about clients until I have an opportunity to hear about it from the clients so I can begin with a positive clean slate. Why else would they leave a former therapist and come to me if there had been a solution? After a less than successful series of therapy sessions, a fresh untainted point of view is necessary. Health care professionals are people like everyone else. After working hard with no results, they also can become frustrated and ready to give up. They can also tell you to stop trying when you should really just find someone new. What we believe in ourselves, from our families, and from professionals causes us to act, productively or destructively.

DON'T FORGET

Being in the Positive Present Moment

There is also another aspect of Tina's story that illustrates the importance of not giving up. People who have aphasia language memory losses become stressed when it is time to recall a word because they expect their memory to fail. Many people do not realize that all memory skills are affected by stress. Under pressure, people who normally remember names well will also forget them. Many useful resources go completely overlooked while someone sits under the fog of pressure, anxiety, stress, or depression. Why? Because the mind is elsewhere and can only be in one place at a time. The place to be is the positive present moment. Think about it. Even the mere suggestion that a name is difficult to remember can cause you to lose a name in a conversation. We've all experienced a moment when we're thinking of a famous person's name in a conversation. The person we're talking to might say, "What's the name of that actor? I can't remember." Even though the name was ready to come off the tip of our tongue only seconds before, the other person's suggestion may cause us to momentarily forget also. This is astoundingly normal in the recollection of facts and details.

Being Shut Down

To begin a program assisting a person redeveloping their memory skills, mere suggestions about how much they have lost or body language reflecting how poorly they are doing will shut them down. All Tina needed was her doctor's report that she was going to get worse and she ignored all evidence to the contrary. She continued to believe the wrong things about herself. Don't we all react this way?

Reacting to Forgetting

So what was she was thinking about when it was time to recall something? First, she wasn't even trying because her belief was that she would not improve. When she might have tried, instead her mind was saying, "I can't do this, I can't do this." You can't be reviewing negative thoughts about how you cannot remember and successfully remember at the same time. You react to the forgetting itself. The mind can only think about one thing or the other. Essentially, this constant negative thinking takes on a life of its own and seems to prove what the doctor originally said was true. Later, after working hard to accept the progress I pointed out to her, she went on to create an active fulfilling life for herself again even to the point of being too busy to return her therapist's phone calls! She teaches music again and is very hard to reach.

Danny's Accident and Working as a Team

Danny's brain injury was due to a car accident. His brain damage and memory loss was also in his speech and language center. His story shows that though head injury and stroke are very different, they produce very similar insults to the brain and require similar time and healing methods. When injury occurs to the brain by stroke or head injury, the brain does not care how the injury occurred. Likewise, we cook in conventional and microwave ovens. The food gets cooked regardless. One method cooks from the outside, the other from the inside.

DON'T FORGET

Brain damage occurs from outside injuries and inside blood clotting problems. The key differences determining recovery will be the level of severity from the injury, its location in the brain, and the treatment and environment where the person lives thereafter.

Working Out—Exercising the Mind

Before we go further into Danny's story, we all know folks who have strengthened their body by physical therapy. So think about how an impaired arm or a leg responds after brain injury and treatment. Unless there is total paralysis, the person usually has to exercise the weakened area. And even in cases like Christopher Reeve's, where total paralysis is perceived, his hard work and his wife's support is changing his situation after spinal cord injury. This is also true for a loss of vocabulary, memory, grammar or articulation loss after lesions to the brain occur. Ongoing study in word related activities is needed to bring results! Think also about how working out improves a healthy body, and remember, it can only do the same for an impaired one. In the same respect, word games keep alert minds sharp. Also appropriate word activities make weakened minds improve. During periods of actual illness, we back off from exercise. The same is true for speaking exercises, until a person is up to it. However, to treat a recovering person as one who is permanently ill when they are simply disabled is wrong. How do we break the cycle of turning a disability into a perpetual, ongoing illness? I hope this book will help all of us to do that. This is the reason for my own efforts to use the name language memory loss instead of just aphasia, which sounds more

CHAPTER SEVEN   JOYCE

like another illness. It's all about attitude if you think about it. We just refuse to let people who are grown up accept the idea that they need some re-education and that's okay.

A Family Who Couldn't Afford Therapy

The proper attitude toward this disability is where Danny's story comes in. He was not a client. His father was my house painter. Every time he came by my house to do another painting job, he would report another story about Danny and how he was doing over several years. He knew I was a speech therapist and always wanted to tell me what was going on and hear my opinion. In essence, the family received my ongoing advice without my presence as a therapist just because we were friends. They could not afford my actual assistance on a regular basis. In the beginning, Danny had some speech therapy, but quickly lost his benefits. Then they were left to their own devices as so many others are.

A Family Project

Danny's family was poor in money, but rich in care and concern for Danny and one another. Over the six-year period I knew this painter, Danny got better. How? From the reports it seems everyone in the family liked taking turns helping him (much like Clay's family reported). I always encouraged the father. I gave him my own ideas here and there for good interventions based on what I heard about Danny, but I never met the boy. Months later, I would hear more. Everyone in Danny's family took pride in Danny's progress. Everyone respected his attempts to improve and wanted to work with him. Was it always that way? Not from what I heard.

The Beginning

In the beginning, Danny's family was not sure Danny would live. When Danny came out of his critical state of health there were the periods of adjustment and acceptance to go through. I was told he was not very happy. I could see the painter was not happy either. In the first year, there always seemed to be sadness, worry and frustration over Danny and his accident and the terminated therapy. But continually, in good times and bad, I always heard that members of the family kept working with Danny.

Six Years Later

At the end of six years, the reports about Danny were quite different from the original reports. Danny had taken a job and was living outside the home. By then it was evident to anyone who heard the story, this family had quite a victory tale that all of them could be proud of. They worked and persevered as a team and reaped a crop in keeping with their efforts and attitudes. Danny's father beamed as he spoke of Danny during the latter years.

Now some of you might believe you cannot do what this family did. Some of you believe you cannot be that patient or give yourself to a problem for that long. But isn't that what you really end up doing with your whole life anyway, working on different projects at different stages? And don't the things you work on usually require a good positive attitude and perseverance to yield any fruit? The difference is that you picked those activities and this one is being forced upon you.

Yes, it is true. No one would ask for brain injuries. Still the character development and pleasure evident in Danny's father as he reported to me on a regular basis was worth more than anything money could ever buy in the joy it produced in that family. I saw that same bond in the families interviewed here who got past the initial acute stage that is so confusing for everyone. Danny's family felt that confusion, but they grew close because of it. So did the families who shared their stories.

Failure through Criticism and Attitude

In my therapeutic experiences, I remember homes that would probably never yield the fruit of Danny's family without serious attitude adjustments. Some spouses sat by critically watching and looking disgusted as they realized their spouses verbal shortcomings. I can recall cases where the spouses actually thought they were being helpful by coming over to criticize the ongoing work and the amount of time it took to do what we were doing. Other spouses sat angrily by full of pain and bitterness over their own inability to adjust. Those people needed to seek caregiver support groups at the very least. Some would never let the person get a word out of their mouth when regular conversation started and the speech therapy was over. And I recall others who simply let the patient's health fail so they never had to really participate in any recovery process. I know some who died and never made it home, but who could have lived many more years.

DON'T FORGET
Regarding Henry vs. *Memento*

What am I saying? Families have everything to do with recovery after serious strokes or head injuries. They play a crucial role in recovery by their willingness to deal with rehabilitative processes. In some families, with a bit more patience and an upbeat attitude, language memory loss persons might not only speak again, but they even live longer and sometimes happier lives. No one is suggesting brain injury should be invoked for helping families get closer, but have you ever seen the movie Regarding Henry played by Harrison Ford? It speaks volumes about families who grow closer because of this type of problem. In other words, there are negatives, but there are also positives in every situation. People amaze me when they share the good, but they do! Without family support, memory loss can turn out more like the movie Memento, not a pretty sight. Insurance issues and lack of proper medical support produced nightmares for every one in that movie! No one should be left to their own devices during serious memory loss like the two displayed in that movie! It's hard to believe our society and medical system could ever come to that, but it has! Go rent these movies to decide for yourself whether they ring of truth.

Without Laura's Support

Do you remember Laura's report about her doctors? They were ready to give up. When she took her stand and insisted on speech therapy, only then did things go the right way. Without Laura's support, Steve might have died in a nursing home and never have regained his

CHAPTER SEVEN — JOYCE

14 years of vitality. The truth is a majority of patients go so much by what the doctors say without appreciating the fact that the doctors can't be sure at the outset that families will be up to this. Therefore, doctors are afraid to suggest patients will get well because they know the family support system is crucial and even if therapy is recommended without that support it may fail. For that reason, I believe doctors cannot offer any guarantees. Unfortunately, many younger doctors of today have not seen the enormous successes of the '60's and '70's and do not want to be held liable if the rehabilitation fails. After dealing with doctors, the majority of families are pretty disgruntled and negative before they even begin any treatments. However, families who stand up for their family members because they have the convictions to try and improve the condition draw the doctor back into the healing mode as Laura did.

Love Saved Danny

So why do I bring up Danny's story now? Well, I did not interview this family or see Danny for therapy. I just casually heard his story over time. The results are wonderful aren't they? Love, warmth and closeness are established. Commitment and family bonds are the glue that put it all together. Danny's story could be very sad like the many others who give up before they begin. The reason Danny succeeded was because he had a supportive family. Isn't that what all of us need no matter what we're going through? Isn't that what will make us or break us all? It was love that saved Danny and a family who was willing and interested in giving him their time and attention. To survive the pains of growth in a difficult world, we all need the kind of support Danny got.

What if the support system is weak at the time of the need? Then so be it. No one is to blame. These are tough issues. The bottom line is, you're reading this book. You had the time, the energy, the inclination, the interest, and the motivation to do so. My dollar is on you being able to support or why would you look into it at all. Does that mean it will be easy? For some it will be surprisingly easy if all the variables are going favorably. For others it will not be easy. Laura was very happy and proud of her accomplishments. Nonetheless, you read her words. The healing process was not so easy and was the hardest at the beginning.

The Difficulties of an Emotional Aphasia

What if you cannot tolerate your situation after trying? Worse, what if your family member or friend has the frustrating angry kind of jargon aphasia sometimes seen. Failing at something as unpredictable as this does not mean you've let your family member down. You are trying to help right now and starting by reading this. You could be very well intentioned and could have done your very best and been met with nothing but negativity from the one you are trying to help and everyone else in your family could be against you for that matter. The successful case depends upon the intertwined dynamics and personalities of the family, the type and severity of language memory loss problem and whether you can work together as a team. Let's face it, someone in trouble with the confusion and instability of a brain injury will not do any healing in the center of adversarial

CHAPTER SEVEN   JOYCE

relationships or heavy frustration and neither will you as a helper. Just remember since brain injury causing aphasia memory loss often affects the emotional center of the brain as well as the language center, you may hear words you never heard before and see tears you've never seen before. Do not be alarmed.

Hopefulness and Grieving

However, though I want you to have hope, I cannot over emphasize the importance of waiting for the person with language memory loss to finish grieving their losses. Allow them to grieve. You will be grieving as well. Allow yourself to grieve, too. If all of you are depressed for a time, remember, that's perfectly fine. Depression is normal at such times and helps all of you take stock as you prepare for some future adjustments. Let the person, yourself and others in the family be depressed. The scripture teaches, "Mourn with those who mourn." That is okay. Wait. The mourning time will pass as you go slowly.

Depression

Fortunately, now that you have heard from the other families, you know they were depressed also, but came through. You also understand how important the family dynamics can be and just how much it helps to surround a language memory loss person with positive attitudes as the depression is moving out. Mostly, just believe in them and remember after the depression the adjusted attitude is: They are becoming something of a language student again, and may not be disabled much at all if physical symptoms are minor.

Let me further highlight the importance of helping the person to believe in themselves enough to move to a studious state. Everyone has gone to school. Parents typically realize that their children need encouragement when they are students in order to continue in their academic challenges. I believe aphasia, for the most part, can best be dealt with when it represents what it really is, a new academic challenge during adulthood, which interrupts other preferred activities and the status quo of relationships. Seen from that perspective, it's just not all that horrible to have to brush up on academic communication skills. People must study all their lives. However, the family's perspective about this is everything. Perspective also determines another speech disorder we ought to discuss here that has similar frustrating dynamics.

To Speak or Not to Speak

In speech therapy circles, it is a well-known fact that when a person stutters, but does not realize they stutter, the sure fire way to make them stutter is to tell them they stutter and to ask them to repeat everything more slowly. You may be surprised to hear that, but it's a fact. One of the first things parents are taught to do about stuttering is to ignore it. Why? Well some scholars call it an approach-avoidance problem. The child has been told he is not speaking properly. Consequently, the next time he decides to speak, he is not really sure he wants to. He is experiencing a conflict between the desire to speak and the desire to be quiet. If you do not really want to speak,

CHAPTER SEVEN   JOYCE

you probably will not speak very well. The same is true for anyone who attempts public speaking. It's great to speak when you feel comfortable, prepared and knowledgeable about your subject, but not when you would rather sit down and listen to someone else. A public speaker who does not wish to speak will also stammer a bit even if he is not a stutterer.

    The point here is to illuminate the seriousness about the beliefs we all carry about aphasia memory loss after the medical community reveals it. We are their audience. Our responses tell them whether to speak or shut down. Their desire to speak must become strong again to overcome the speaking difficulties and rebuild the failed system. Someone must sincerely desire to hear from them again and let them believe they fully expect them to eventually turn their speech around. If that element is missing, I venture to say we give in to the diagnosis of aphasia to the detriment of the person. We give up and make it become the stronger reality until it is ingrained as a habit difficult to change.

Negative therapy reports can interfere with your benefits

    Remember, the ideal situation is to have the speech therapist work at least twice weekly with your family member for what could be a year or more, which is rather expensive unless covered by insurance. No one is suggesting you can replace speech therapy, but even if you have exhausted your insurance resources, no therapist wants to see your person with memory loss stagnate for that reason. The day the therapist says there is nothing else that can be done is the day you need a new therapist. Most may not be willing to admit this. Instead, they may report that it is time to terminate therapy because they have exhausted their ideas and energies. Be careful! Your insured therapy services may permanently drop if such a report is written. My advice is: If it has only been a few short weeks or months and the person is no better, persuade the speech therapist to refer your family member to another therapist if they can. That way, benefits are not terminated because of negative therapy notes. It is possible you may lose your additional insured services because of their unpromising report. I would encourage them to make positive notes and recommendations. And don't get me wrong, there are times when the therapist must stop. However, I believe people with language memory loss will progress again even after therapists are gone if the circumstances are conducive to improvement—maybe not right away, but at some point. The problem for therapists is continually coming back to check on the fluctuating periods of progress. Being paid for it can be rather difficult as well. This is what the therapists should be allowed to do in the future. Doctors and insurance plans should more readily support the ongoing reevaluation process. Someday, maybe?

Plan

Now, for those of you who have already gotten all the insured therapy services you can get and are ready for a new formula and believe you have some of what it takes to help a language memory loss person get this ball rolling; if you like computers go to the Internet and pull up www.google.com then set your search engine to "aphasia," "stroke," "head injury," "brain tumor," etc. you will be able to find support programs and some Internet

CHAPTER SEVEN   JOYCE

software programs like Parrotsoftware.com or even electronic language and vocabulary device at www.aphasia.com very inexpensively. If you prefer, simply review the workbook offers in Appendix C and the ideas in Appendix D. There you will be able to choose from 10 thick workbooks full of practice opportunities for recovering memory loss to order from the publishers and many tips. Before you decide which items to purchase, if you can, talk to your last memory loss professional about your choices and their usefulness for your friend or family member. You can also make an appointment with me at: www.dontforgetmemoryloss.com. Hopefully, you will figure out where to begin by getting a bit of outside help, but even a teacher knows about readiness. You can begin to do what you do understand by reviewing ideas in Appendix C and D. Every memory loss problem is a little different.

    If you feel you do not have what it takes to get started, are out of funds for services, don't want your previous therapist back, then call another licensed speech pathologist. Ask him to come over and help you pick out for someone in your family to practice using with the language memory loss person or to pick out some practice work he or she could possibly do alone, maybe by computer. Have the therapist review the software programs and books you are planning to buy just to be sure they are the most useful ones for you. When he or she sees how determined you are, he or she may even barter some of their services for some of yours. If you can afford to pay out of pocket, you may decide to buy some extra sessions not covered by insurance from that speech pathologist. Then ask him or her to let you or your family members or friends watch the therapy if the memory loss

DON'T FORGET

person does not mind, then you will have opportunity to see how to and how not to help your family member. If he or she realizes you have used all your services and are asking for helpful advice because you cannot afford more than that, they will assist you in developing a plan and they will advise and assist you again in the future when you need more help.

Sing Songs and Read Audio Books Aloud

That understood, you are setting up a long-term curriculum with the help of a therapist if possible. For minimal costs, the therapist can come in for periodic ongoing reevaluations and maintenance especially if your family member is having no problem working on the computer, in the workbooks, or doing the other activities listed in Appendix C and D at the levels the therapist suggested. Some simple practice methods are very elegant. For example, not everyone is ready for this step, but many language memory loss persons like reading books out loud while listening to the same book read by an actor or actress on a tape player. Others like singing along to old songs, even in the shower. These activities are two examples of things patients like to do alone once they realize how much it helps to hear their own words, sung or read. As stated before, the Internet also provides huge independent resources. If you have too much difficulty implementing these ideas, then investigate the addition of a family therapist to help you and the speech pathologist lay out a plan for you and your family during this time of recovery from language memory loss.

CHAPTER SEVEN　　　　　　　　**JOYCE**

Pick Appropriate Materials

You'll eventually learn what's too much and what's not enough. You'll make mistakes. Remember two things. If the level of work seems childish to you, first, do not allow the language memory loss person to notice that you think the work is childish. They already know that and are often embarrassed about it. Pick adult looking materials with large bold fonts to help with their vision problems and your own if you are past 50. Many vision difficulties can occur with language memory loss. Second, remember that even though the work you are doing with your language memory loss person may appear simple to you, synaptic movements in the neural pathways are connecting. Missing files and data are being found in the brain. They are formatting new neural connections to the data. The information is still on the hard drive. It takes basic vocabulary input and repetition to reopen the connections and find the missing files. Watch other lost information reappear afresh as you plug along and be encouraged. This recovery happens all the time and is normal as long as there is some stimulation. At first, it looks like a lot of replication, but you will see, you are reestablishing the connections, the wiring, and the associations. You are rebuilding by finding connections to the old information. At first it will feel like you have to reenter all the data, later, you'll realize that was not so as many words flood back into use by the language memory loss person. Most words come back easily after the recall of an associated similar word.

DON'T FORGET

Support Groups

What if it is all just too difficult? Remember, you will feel that way at times and will need to take care of yourself and your frustrations as well. Certainly you will feel that way at first. The situation changes over time. Now and then while you are working the plan, call the speech pathologist or go see a family therapist. Take advantage of the many stroke, head injury, brain tumor, and aphasia support groups out there. Many are listed under Appendix C especially ones available through www.aphasia.org or those specific to a particular illness. Many use separate groups for caregivers and language memory loss persons to give each opportunities to discuss how they are dealing with certain aspects of language memory loss. Both integrated and separated groups are helpful.

If your speech therapist will not call you back or help you with your plan, please, find another one. Therapists are a lot like money managers. If one won't work and you need one, obviously you have to go find one who understands the type of investment strategy you want to use. If you do find a good one, remember, therapists are just temporary. You need ongoing support for your plan because this kind of neurological damage repairs over long periods of time and only you and your family can keep the language memory loss person on track and on task like these families did.

Body Language

The motivation and desire of the language memory loss person to work will be closely tied to the attitudes they see around them. When one loses the ability to speak, they naturally begin to pay a lot more attention to the gestures, body language, sighs, groans, and vocal tones of those around them. The truth is, your language memory loss family member probably understands a lot more about what is going on by watching your facial expressions, hearing you tone of voice and watching your body language then you realize.

You—the Default Healer

When you think of them as being in school for the next few years, remember, just as you make sure a child gets to school, you can help find ways to properly stimulate this healing process and take care of yourself at the same time. If you cannot find anyone who works as hard as you do for your loved one, guess what? You are not alone. Lots of people are becoming the default healers. Over the long haul, you are the best ongoing source of therapeutic assistance for your language memory loss person. Would you give up on your investments and not try to figure out what to do with your funds if all the money managers disappeared, I do not think so. Keep your priorities straight and do not give up in these more crucial matters.

When you are both up to it and successful days increase, try to learn what they are capable of doing. Then, based on that--set the person with memory loss up to the table. Hand him or her a workbook and pen. Turn on the computer or tape player. Load the software or cassette. When you want them to read aloud to audio books, read along with them at first if it encourages them.

DON'T FORGET

Or you can purchase a hand held PDA or lingraphica device (Appendix C & D).

Leave the activities alone when they're frustrated and don't want them. But whatever it is you and the therapists you've found have devised as best for your family member, just keep on trying to do it like you would with an ornery teenager if that's how it feels until they want to do the work as much as you want them to. This is just one more life challenge like any other! And remember, it is because of your bond that you may be the best one for this job! If you worked well with this person in the past on projects, it will probably still be possible to do this project in the same spirit.

If You Think You Can't You're Right—
If You Think You Can You're Right

So guess what? Right now I believe you can answer the question of whether you can be a team in your family or join in and help a friend who has this disorder or not. Why? Because if you think you can, you're right, and if you think you can't, you're right! The value of hopefulness and confidence is very evident in the recovery stories you read here. The lack of hope if there was even a chance at recovery devastated family functioning. The presence of hope even when desired normality was never reached was still better than the alternative. The professionals in the stories you read would not counsel the families to continue their speaking pursuits, but all the families mentioned here succeeded save one, whose daughter was uninformed, stressed out and new to the problem when I interviewed her.

CHAPTER SEVEN   **JOYCE**

Placed in this same circumstance, I want you to know recovery is more than possible in most cases, but it's your part that tips the scales to make that so. No one will tell you ahead if you are going to be able to take that role. Your desire to make similar attempts to these valiant families will hold the answer to your futures. Many of them reaped incredible benefits and blessings. If you are a person of faith, you might consider prayer or meditation as it helped those who did have that belief including Tina and Bob and Kay.

To all of you, I believe you can probably help your loved one with memory loss better than any one else in the world we live in today. As one woman who thanked me years later said, 'I didn't like what you told me I needed to do. I didn't want to accept this, but God used it to make us better people and to make me into a better person.' And then she thanked me with a sense of pride and accomplishment. Believe me, that was not where she began! Each person comes to grips with this in their own unique fashion gaining that understanding along the way. These are simply the people I met who succeeded.

Final Note

Please contact *www.dontforgetmemoryloss.com* to make an online appointment or to share a memory loss story that may appear in future publications or on the site. Those long-term memory loss stories are really important for others to know about. So tell me your success stories and also offer wheat grass and other nutritional testimonies at dontforget@bellsouth.net, and be sure to add a line giving me permission to publish them later.

DON'T FORGET

Memory loss recipes and other helpful information will also be featured regularly at the website.

Now review Appendices C, D, and E, full of the treatments and resources I've already suggested. And as the saying goes—never, never, never give up. Some people do have to slow down and wait for more growth to come, but never give up entirely. Just take breaks. Before you stop trying, please make an on line appointment with me at Dr. Phil's referral site mytherapynet.com. A link will connect you from www.dontforgetmemoryloss.com. Just log on, enroll, and then enter my name under your therapist choice.

In my clinical private practice experiences, I can hardly even recall a case I did not see succeed to new levels unless the patient was transferred out of my care or insurance stopped our work. Throughout, I maintained this same attitude. There were times when persons did not feel up to it because they had other things like physical therapy taking their energies. Ten minutes every other day then, but please keep reattempting on a regular basis and one day it will look different. Any and all of you have my encouragement and God bless you and your family!

                              Thank you and don't forget!

Dr. Jill

Part Three

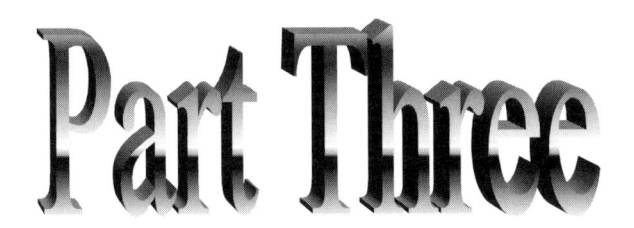

Appendix A

Memory Loss Glossary with Subcategories

Appendix B

The Different Types of Language Memory Loss

Appendix C

Treatment and Internet Resources for Memory-Training, Therapy Books, Support Groups, and Memory Loss Plans

Appendix D

Tips for Serious Language Memory Loss and Memory-training

Appendix E

RDA of Memory Vitamin Nutrients Compared to Wheat Grass Product

Memory Support Health Food Store Shopping List

DON'T FORGET

Appendix A

Memory Loss Glossary with Subcategories

Amnesia: Inability to remember experiences before a head trauma (retrograde) or one's upcoming after a head trauma (anterograde). The latter also affects learning of new information. These persons can also experience aphasic symptoms described throughout this glossary.

Aphasia: Aphasia is a language memory loss disturbance that crosses all language modalities. The four main language modalities affected include: understanding spoken language (reception), reading, talking, (expression), and writing (Schuell, 1974). This glossary contains the numerous characteristics of aphasia unless otherwise specified.

Receptive Aphasias: These are decoding disorders or difficulties in understanding and comprehension (De Vito, 1970). ". . . aphasic patients show some impairment of ability to understand spoken language. This impairment is characterized by reduced comprehension of spoken words, by reduction of the auditory retention span, and usually, in addition, by some impairment of the ability to discriminate between similar auditory patterns" (Schuell, 174, p. 93). The inability to discriminate between identical and dissimilar auditory signals has been called "auditory discrimination." Sometimes, this discrimination can be so severely impaired in a patient that ". . . much of the language they hear is virtually unintelligible to them" (Schuell, 1974, p. 93). This has been clearly demonstrated to be "not related to hearing loss but instead to interferences with the processing of the complex patterns of acoustic stimuli that language presents to the ear" (Schuell, 1974, p. 92). "Comprehension is not an all-or none phenomenon. Many aphasic patients comprehend frequently used words but fail to understand words used less often" (Benson, 1985, p. 24).

Expressive Aphasias: These are encoding disorders or difficulties in verbalizing and speaking (De Vito, 1970). First, aphasic patients have difficulty in "word finding" as a result of their weak lexicon. Their speech is also fragmented and disjointed due to their "anomia" (explained below) and reduced attention span. Patients with severe "word finding" problems talk in single words first, followed later by phrases and short sentences (Schuell, 1974).

Agnosia: "Agnosia" bears resemblance to the difficulties of poor discrimination and poor reception just discussed, but implies a more total "absence of knowledge" (Reitan & Wolfson, 1992, p. 295). In aphasia, this is a " . . . impairment of ability to recognize the symbolic meaning of stimulus material" (Bauer & Rubens, 1985; Reitan & Wolfson, 1992, p. 295). "Auditory agnosia" applies " . . . to the total inability to differentiate all varieties of sound," from fine speech sounds to grosser environmental noises (Spreen et al., 1995, p. 430). This also occurs in auditory discrimination, but at a less severe level. Other "agnosias" also bear mentioning. "Visual agnosia" affects reading ability and "tactile agnosia" affects the reception of

DON'T FORGET

information touched and felt by the skin in and about the environment.

Dysgnosia: "In contrast to agnosia, dysgnosia represents a partial rather than complete loss of the symbolic significance of information reaching the brain" (Reitan & Wolfson, 1992, p. 301).

Anomia: This is a form of aphasia in which the ability to retrieve common vocabulary words is affected and is also referred to as a "word finding difficulty" (Benson, 1985, p. 24). This aspect of aphasia most makes an aphasic individual like a visitor in his or her own culture. He or she is familiar with the language and often understands much more than others realize, but cannot find the words. Again, he or she is like "someone trying to use a language that he or she once knew but now recalls only imperfectly" (Schuell, 1974, p. 87). Anomia is undoubtedly the most common and well-known linguistic difficulty among aphasics and is caused by the overall reduction of available vocabulary. Also, because of the reduced verbal attention span, "The aphasic patient can only hold a limited number of words in his [or her] mind at a time" (Schuell, 1974, p. 90). Words that are most frequently used in the language will be the "words aphasic patients can use first," recover most easily, and use most often thereafter (Schuell, 1974, p. 90). "Anomia" occurs across all language modalities: understanding, reading, talking, and writing (Schuell, 1974).

Dysnomia: [Partial] "Impairment of the ability to name objects, resulting from a brain lesion" (Reitan & Wolfson, 1992, p. 301). Again, as in the use of the terms aphasia/dysphasia, this term, "dysnomia", could probably be used more accurately than "anomia" in describing that condition. However, "anomia" has been the commonly accepted term used to describe partial loss of the ability to name objects.

Apraxia and Dysarthria: These are motor disorders and may coexist with aphasia, but are not due to aphasia. The muscle weakness of "dysarthria" or the lack of voluntary motor control of "apraxia," which has been described as an "inability to carry out motor activities on verbal command," may be occurring simultaneously with the aphasia (Benson, 1985, p. 24). This is not to be confused with any forms of paralysis to the speaking mechanism. Although "dysarthria" and "apraxia" are a result of the stroke, these disorders can exist alone or in combination with the aphasia. Typically, "right hemispheric lesions" are responsible for motor deficits and "do not cause aphasia in most people" (Kertesz, 1985, p. 48). In addition, the level of impairment of the articulation affected by "dysarthria" and "apraxia" is "not correlated with the severity of language deficit" (Schuell, 1974, p. 97).

Alexia: Loss of the ability to read and understand the symbolic significance of words. This is more commonly and appropriately coined "dyslexia."

DON'T FORGET

Dyslexia: "Impairment (due to a brain lesion) of reading ability and the understanding of the symbolic significance of words. A symptom of [aphasia] dysphasia" (Reitan & Wolfson, 1992, p. 301). All aphasic patients will show some reduction of reading vocabulary and in verbal attention span. This will affect retention and integration of what they read. Some patients will also have marked impairment of "visual discrimination" (Schuell, 1974, p. 94). This could cause confusion in reading between letters and words that look alike. This is a form of "fine visual discrimination." As severity increases, "gross visual discrimination" could be affected and cause patients to not recognize one letter as different from another or to see words or lines on a page. "Spatial disorientation", a loss of sense of direction or position, may cause him or her not to keep his or her place and follow well while reading (Schuell, 1974, p. 94). Also, with "visual field defect" or "visual field neglect" the patient may be unable to see well either to the left or to the right (Schuell, 1974, p. 94) in attempting to read written material.

Acalculia: A disturbance of the ability to do mathematics as related to the loss of memory and communication skills.

Agraphia/Dysgraphia: "A loss of ability to form letters when writing, resulting when a brain fail to understand words used less often" (Benson, 1985, p. 24).

Agrammatism: A disturbance of the ability to properly use well-known grammatical forms. One common example is the confusion between pronouns informing others of gender, like using 'him' for 'her' or 'she' for 'he,' etc.

Astereognosis: "Inability to identify objects through the sense of touch" (Reitan & Wolfson, 1992, p. 296).

Dysstereognosis: "Impairment of ability [a partial inability] to recognize objects through touch" (Reitan & Wolfson, 1992, p. 301).

Dementia: "Significant deterioration of intellectual and cognitive functions (Reitan & Wolfson, 1992, p. 300)

Associated deficits that often overlap aphasia: Dysarthria (weakness of articulatory musculature), apraxia (inability to articulate voluntarily), dysphagia (difficulty in swallowing), agnosias (lost knowledge), right-left confusion, constructional deficits, visual-spatial neglect, amnesia disorders, dementia, and frontal lobe deficits (Knox, 1985; Reitan & Wolfson, 1992).

Jargon: Connected speech utterances having little or no meaning.

Neologisms: Made up words.

Paraphasias: Word substitutions; similar sound to target.

Perseveration: Abnormal and severe disability in repetition of words or parts of words; like stuttering.

DON'T FORGET

Appendix B

The Different Types of Language Memory Loss

Broca's Aphasia: Broca's *aphasia* is a non-fluent (expressive) anterior brain disorder characterized by "intact comprehension, but never fully intact," and poor verbal output (Benson, 1985, p. 29; Damasio, 1981; Kertesz & McCabe, 1977; Peach, 1987). The patients are usually able to repeat the names of objects and use nouns mostly in the singular number. Abstract parts of speech that are more "grammatical," like articles, prepositions, adverbs, and conjunctions are not commonly used, the patients are restricted to the key necessary words for communication (Gardner, 1975, p. 63) and also have high rates of recovery (Damasio, 1981; Kertesz & McCabe, 1977; Peach, 1987). This is most likely relative to their high levels of comprehension, which are particularly helpful to them in achieving success in the therapeutic setting. They respond well to various cues, such as stimulating the first sound of the next word being attempted, vocabulary words to picture associations, and filling in the blanks of open-ended completion phrases (Gardner, 1975). Automatic language activities also flow with ease such as singing, counting, repeating well-known verses such as the Pledge to the Flag, the alphabet, memorized prayers, etc.

Wernicke's Aphasia: Wernicke's *aphasia* (receptive *aphasia*) involves poor comprehension of language and is the complication of *paraphasias* (semantic substitutions) and *jargon,* so much so, it has also been referred to as *jargon aphasia* (Benson, 1985). Such a patient can continue to use *jargon* for up to two years prior to improving. Another case did not improve for 8 months until visual stimuli were used as the only method of retraining. When *jargon* is not used heavily, the *aphasia* has an increased chance of improving with time, but the patient could continue to have *anomic* (naming) and *semantic* (meaning) errors (Kertesz & McCabe, 1977). The *jargon* speech of a Wernicke's *aphasic* patient can be confused with the *"word salad"* of a psychotic individual. The difference is that the *aphasia* patient's lesion may heal given time and retraining in ways to discriminate and reproduce correct language. Gardner (1975) reports that the brain can actually develop new neural pathways on which to relearn and comprehend the meaning of conversational words (pp. 68-69). Nonetheless, due to the emotionality added by the effect of using jargon, usually unknowingly, a Wernicke's patient is in danger of being *"misplaced . . . [into the care of] . . . mental health services"* (Benson, 1985, p. 31).

Conduction Aphasia: Conduction *aphasic* patients have severe difficulty with *perseveration* (abnormal and severe disability in repetition) and make many articulatory errors as well as *neologisms,* (made up words) and *paraphasias* (semantic substitutions). Their comprehension is usually good and they are relatively fluent with possibilities for a full recovery (Benson, 1985, p. 33; Kertesz & McCabe, 1977). They respond well to language activities to improve their difficulties.

DON'T FORGET

***Anomic Aphasia*:** Anomic *aphasia* affects the mildest of language impairments: The inability to recall names with ease. Even when improvement occurs, some naming difficulty and circumlocutory speech may remain. However, these patients often recover completely. Sometimes *"alexia,"* which is disturbed reading, and *"agraphia,"* which is disturbed writing, are problems for the anomic *aphasia* patients and affect their employment prospects (Benson, 1985; Kertesz & McCabe, 1977). Retraining through vocabulary building stimulated via all possible sensate processes is highly successful.

***Global Aphasia*:** Global *aphasia* refers to a total loss of language, in which both expressive and receptive language of all varieties is seriously impaired (Benson, 1985; Damasio, 1981; Peach, 1987). These patients understand little or nothing, speak only in stereotypical utterances, and as a rule, have limited recoveries (Kertesz & McCabe, 1977). Global *aphasia* represents the most severe form of *Aphasia* and has the poorest prognosis. However, global *aphasic* patients have been known to make dramatic recoveries with rigorous treatment, especially when stimulation is offered during the initial six months to a year after the disorder ensues. The probability of improvement often seems limited due to their apparent lack of response, but ongoing attempts at language stimulation can be rewarded suddenly and significantly. However, there are never any guarantees and many researchers believe that the majority of global patients do not improve immensely. As researcher and therapist, I concur, global aphasia is the most difficult type of aphasia to conquer, but hasten to add, ongoing rigorous treatment, in spite of periods where there is seemingly little response, is often the missing variable in the equation that could correct this form of aphasia. The reason for this is apparent. There are no guarantees of success, however, there are no guarantees of failure either. Therefore, the family must choose how to press on rigorously and for how long the rigor is feasible. Again, the first six months to a year remains the most important. Quitting, for me, would not be an option until at least six months of retraining had been attempting five days per week.

DON'T FORGET

Appendix C

Treatment and Internet Resources for Memory-Training, Treatment Books, Support Groups, and Memory Loss Plans

Aurelia, J. (1980). *Aphasia therapy manual.* Danville, IL: The Interstate Printers & Publishers, Inc.

Bassett, Lucinda. (2000). *Attacking Anxiety and Depression.* Oak Harbor, OH: The Midwest Center. 800-944-9428. Epilepsy, anxiety, depression recommendation.

Brubaker, S. (1982). *Sourcebook for Aphasia: A guide to family activities and community resources.* Detroit, MI: Wayne State University Press.

Brubaker, S. (1983). *Workbook for reasoning skills.* Detroit, MI: Wayne State University Press.

Brubaker, S. (1984). *Workbook for language skills.* Detroit, MI: Wayne State University Press.

Brubaker, S. (1985). *Workbook for Aphasia: Revised edition.* Detroit, MI. Wayne State University

Brubaker, S. (1987). *Workbook for cognitive skills.* Detroit, MI: Wayne State University Press.

Keith, R. (1984a). *Speech and language rehabilitation: A workbook for the neurologically impaired,* Volume I. Danville, IL: The Interstate Printers and Publishers, Inc.

Keith, R. (1984b). *Speech and language rehabilitation: A workbook for the neurologically impaired,* Volume 2. Danville, IL: The Interstate Printers and Publishers, Inc.
Kilpatrick, K. (1979). *Therapy guide for the adult with language and speech disorders: Volume II, advanced stimulus materials.* Akron, OH: Visiting Nurse Service.

Kilpatrick, K., & Jones, C. (1977). *Therapy guide for the adult with language and speech disorders: Volume I, a selection of stimulus materials.* Akron, OH: Visiting Nurse Service.

Peterson, C. (1981). *Conversation starters.* Danville, IL: The Interstte Printers & Publishers.

Stryker, S. (1981). *Speech after stroke: A manual for the speech pathologist and the family member.* Springfield, IL: Charles C. Thomas.

www.abta.org American Brain Tumor of America. Review for support groups and information. 800-886-2282.

www.bisusa.org Brain Injury Association of America. Review for support groups and information. 608-819-0742.

www.aphasia.com Lingraphicare device—for assistance with language memory loss.

DON'T FORGET

www.aphasia.ca Canadian program

www.aphasiahope.org Aphasia Hope Foundation

www.aphasia.org Review multiple programs and find support groups offered by the National Aphasia Association. 800-638-8255.

www.alz.org Alzheimer's Disease and Related Disorders Association. Review for support groups and information. 800-272-3900.

www.careguide.com Children of Aging Parents. 800-227-7294.

www.ec-online.net Alzheimer's information.

www.epilepsyfoundation.org Epilepsy information and support. 800-332-1000

www.gusinc.com Handheld PDA computers handy for recall and word finding.

www.innovativespeech.com.html Helpful support group and computer information for memory loss.

www.mealsonwheels.org Meals to homebound. 616-531-9909.

www.medicare.gov Medicare Hotline.
800-638-6833

www.nho.org Hospice Helpline. 800-658-8898.
Referrals for the terminally ill.

www.ncoa.org/nadsa/ Adult day care referrals
800-424-9046/ 202-479-6682

www.parrotsoftware.com for fine memory loss and cognitive skills computer software programs

www.ssww.com AdaptAbility—Products for Independent Living. 800-243-9232.

www.stroke.org National Stroke Association. Review information. Locate local support groups. 800-787-6537.

www.toastmasters.ogg Toastmasters International. 949-858-8255.

www.questia.com a very helpful search library with language memory loss tools

www.uk.connect.org Australian program

DON'T FORGET

Appendix D

25 Tips for Serious Language Memory Loss and Memory-training

1. These tips get progressively more challenging at the end so wait and use them as they become realistic. Put them out of your mind if you find they are too difficult until a later time. Build up to them slowly.

2. Do not assume the language challenged person cannot read. Lost reading skills will come back especially when reading cues are used around the house and the person is able to get up and go about. At first they may tell you to take cues away because they cannot read anyway. Do not take them away. You will have to learn to ignore some things they say during this process.

3. Look at each other when you speak to avoid normal hearing loss problems of aging from interfering with communication that is already difficult. Do not attempt to speak to the person from another room except to let them know you are nearby. Look at them in the face when you tell them where you will be going.

4. As much as it is practical for you, express out loud when you can be heard by the language memory loss person: a) What you are doing, and b) What they are doing as you go about your daily activities. Eventually let them be the one to play this role. They may fall into it naturally as they repeat you. If they don't after a few weeks ask them to do it with you.

5. Noun vocabulary building. Initially label each of the items around the house with the written word that matches it as one might do in a foreign country while learning a new language. Use a colorful marker like red or blue for this project. Computer labels from office supply stores work well.

6. Use checklists constantly around the house in bathrooms and by the doors. Make sure the letters on the lists are abnormally large, bold, and preferably black to distinguish these from the noun vocabulary builders in #5. Double space lists and keep them short and to the point. Check off items on to do lists with them as you eat breakfast or leave the house for different daily activities. Have a list within reading view for them when they are seated in the car or bathroom. They may not follow it at first, but it will remind them to put on their seat belt, to check the door and be sure it is closed properly, or to zip up their purse or pants!

7. Label directions on things like fan switches if they are similar to the light switches. It may be helpful to keep items like light switches, air conditioners and remote controls labeled permanently. Mark things like "on," "off," "hot," and "cold" with arrows. Don't forget to label the faucets somehow. Make the labels large and bold. Let the person remove them when they show they obviously no longer have any need for these

DON'T FORGET

memory markers. Do not discuss the wisdom of these ideas. Just do them. If these insult them they may remove them prematurely while they still need them.

8. For the person unable to recall words of familiar items in the home, once the person can walk, you can number your labels around the house from #5 and then make a simple tape recording stating the number followed by each of the words clearly into the microphone. Then keep the cassette and a lightweight battery operated cassette player handy for them to go around the house and match up the numbered recording to the numbered labels. Leave small 10 second spaces of time between the items progressing in numerical order on the recording. Then as they desire and at first with your prompting, go around the house and match up the recorded words to the labels and numbered items. They can then begin repeating the words to the best of their ability. Try to keep the numbered items in an order so that it is easy to walk from one item to the next in order. Complete a room full of items before starting another room. Go to the next room and record all the words in that room, which are labeled. This gives the person a chance to repeat the vocabulary words while looking at the item named with the written word that matches it.

9. If the language memory loss person is not capable of moving about the house, gather pictures and labels from books listed in Appendix C. Stryker's book has

many. Keep a list of words you have reviewed and read them aloud slowly every other week always with a matched picture and the written word also. Perhaps they will say them also. If they reject this activity, try to make a recording so they will at least listen to the recorder if you set it up in numerical order as suggested above.

10. Make many separate bulletin or poster boards filled with photographs of old friends, family, neighbors, hospital staff, support group friends, and other people you see regularly. Use photo album sheets if you like. Label the names clearly. Separate and label sections and each photograph. Hang these or place them around the house. Keep family photos with family photos then above the group of photos place the label "FAMILY." Do the same with old friends, new friends, neighbors, professionals, etc. An orderly organized presentation helps! Practice and review the names on each board regularly, asking questions as you go and looking for complete responses if possible. EG. "Who is that?" Response: "That is Suzy." "Tell me more about Suzy." Follow guidelines of upcoming #17 if you have difficulty with complete responses.

11. Carry a magnifier light with you for quick reading light and magnification for the person with memory loss to use above and beyond spectacles for times when you are out of the house together. This will keep them more in tune with social and outside functions and activities. This number (800-306-5300) carries an inexpensive one. Even if the person cannot read, the light and magnification will encourage them to try.

DON'T FORGET

Show them how to use it. If they cannot use it, hold it over the item they are attempting to read on a menu for example. Isolation of words in this style can be a wonderful tool as you will see it separates the item requiring focused attention from the other items. If these magnifiers are not large enough for your person to use, find magnification sheets sold on the market with school supplies (8.5X11) and continue to isolate words in reading as needed by using paper to block on coming reading so focus can occur on each word slowly. This method of presentation will help reading projects at home also. Therapists use these regularly.

12. Have large marker pens or chalk available in the beginning. The smaller ones are harder to handle after a head injury or stroke. Find a small chalkboard or other large hard surface for the language memory loss person to write notes to themselves if they desire to. Large yellow pads with large pens or pencils also work well. The person can also practice tracing over the alphabet to improve their writing skills. You can get a large copy of the printed or cursive alphabet. Pick the style they used in the past. If they printed, find a printed alphabet. If they wrote in cursive, find a cursive alphabet. Or better yet, get both and let them choose. These are easily found in school supply shops around town. If they do not begin to use these items or tended more toward their computer, just keep these items available or offer them an open word processing document in their computer set with a large 14-20

point font so they can jot a note down when they get up the nerve to attempt it. When they are alone they will try to use these things if they are not made to feel childish for doing so. Later they can trace the words they find around the house on their yellow pad, if you have labeled the items in the house as you really ought to. Ask them to do this.

13. Draw maps of your neighborhood, church or places you frequent for regular review before going out to those places. At the early stages hang the maps up and label the areas appropriately. You may wish to start with a simple drawing of the map to the hospital clinic, placing the names of familiar sites along the way for identification. Then you could draw another map of the hallway you travel to get to support groups or to see the doctor. Label the elevators and the buildings. Put the name of the street and the building on your map. Review these as you travel during your outing.

14. Take a two-minute walk twice daily just to get out and about and increase oxygen to the brain if the person with aphasia is able and the doctor approves. Increase the time when the person is able. Physically able persons should increase exercise to at least 30 minutes per day.

15. Sing old songs well known in the past out loud with them. Keep lyrics to songs of their generation handy. Play CD's or cassettes of their songs with song sheets to read and sing along. Encourage them to sing in the shower as well. Any refreshment and mental

DON'T FORGET

connections of this type increases memory. Accessing as many forms of sensation as possible in an activity always increases the mental imaging on the brain.

16. Play fill in the blanks games. EG: "Three cheers for the red, white and _____." Numerous versions of this and other helpful word games are available in the Brubaker, Keith and Stryker books and on the www.parrotsoftware.com website. (See Appendix C).

17. Use pneumonic devices to increase concepts such as verb usage. Playing a simple version of charades, act out any action. Place three index cards in front of the person. Each card represents a word they need to say in this game. Act out "singing" for example. Then pause and say, "What was I doing?" The answer of course is – "You were singing." Let them take a turn if they like and go back and forth.

18. If they are willing, play Simon Says. This reminds language memory loss persons of the name associated with their actions and is the reason I asked you to talk about what you are doing every day if you can. Play Simon Says and other games only when they are in the mood to do such things and have begun to enjoy this process. Always put away ideas that make them feel foolish and bring up at another time.

19. Review geography, history or other fields the person knew well and would want to know again.

Relearning words from fields they mastered is especially important to regaining their self-esteem.

20. Listen to word game shows. Create your own family versions of Trivial Pursuit using the words around the house the person has learned! Occasionally try to play word games like Scrabble. Let the person just listen or watch until they become interested.

21. Have the language memory loss person read out loud from a book while listening to the same cassette version of audio books. If they want to listen to audio books without reading aloud that is also a good activity later after they are recovering somewhat. The best activities always include vocalizing of some sort. If they only want to read aloud the first and last page of every chapter that would even be helpful. Some is better than none and rules are made to be broken. No activities should be forced upon them, just encouraged.

22. While you are encouraging, you may hear rebuttals and arguments. Leave the opportunities within their reach and let them use them as they choose. If the activities are ones you need to be involved in and they refuse to participate, back away or ask another family member or friend to try. Could be you will need some more encouragement from a speech therapist or family therapist.

23. Get a computer and hook it up to www.parrotsoftware.com or order a lingraphica device if you prefer it. A special laptop computer is

DON'T FORGET

available at www.aphasia.com. A handheld PDA version is sold at www.gusinc.com.

24. Support Groups. Get out and go to support groups with the NAA, NSA, head injury, or Alzheimer's support associations. Phone numbers are in Appendix C. The web addresses for the main ones are www.aphasia.org, www.alz.org, www.stroke.org, www.biausa.org, and www.abta.org. The memory loss person can go to one group and the closest family member, friend, or caregiver can go to another, or you can stay together. See Appendix C for details and phone numbers.

25. Outside Education Opportunities. Plan ahead and go to your local Toastmaster's meetings after speech has returned. Apply at www.toastmasters.org. This will definitely sharpen speaking skills when and if the person feels up to it and likes the idea. Check in with the person in charge before attending to find out the best times to attend and how to prepare. College classes, adult education, and community groups are other viable options at the latter stages. See Appendix C.

APPENDICES   JOYCE

Appendix E

Recommended Daily (RDA) Minimum of Vitamins and Minerals and Daily Recommended Intake (DRI) compared to Wheat Grass contents in one and three tablespoons. Read RDA% column to reveal estimated percentages in 3 tablespoons of wheat grass.

*Memory Support Health Food Store Shopping List (See p. 248).

VITAMINS	MINIMUM RDA/DRI	Wheat Grass in 1 tbsp.	RDA% for 3 tbsp.
BetaCarotene/Vit. A	5000 IU	2500-5000 IU	50-90%
Vit. E	30 IU	4mg/775-960mcg	27%
Vit. C	60 mg	20-60mg	99-300%
Vit. B1/thiamine	1.5 mg	.4 mg-33mcg	75%
Vit. B2/riboflavin	1.7 mg	.8mg/ 660-780 mcg	102%
Vit. B3/niacin	1.8 mg	4 mg/ 642-756mcg	33-200%
Vit. B5/pantothenic acid	4.7 mg	91-108mcg	6%
Vit. B6 pyrodoxine	2 mg	.13mg/ 99-117 mcg	18%
Vit. B8/9 folic acid	400 mcg	63-90 mcg	67-90%
Vit. B12 cobalamine	6 mcg	15 mcg	10%
Vit. K		90-105 mcg	180%
Vit. H biotin	30 mcg	12 mcg	40%
Choline	no RDA 250 mg	15-133 mg	20-160%
Vitamin D	400 IU	Trace	

DON'T FORGET

MINERALS	MINIMUM RDA	1 tbsp. Wheat Grass	3tbsp./RDA% Wheat Grass
Calcium	1.0 g	45 mg	11%
Phosphorus	400 mg	42 mg	28%
Iodine	150 mcg	24 mcg	45%
Iron	10-30mg	2610 mcg	40%
Magnesium	350 mg	11.7 mg	10%
Copper	2 mg	51 mcg	
Lutein		3 mg	
Lycopene		75 mcg	
Zinc	15 mg	186 mcg	120%
Selenium:	DRI 200mcg	16.5 mcg	58%
Xeazanthin		700 mcg	

AMINO ACIDS	1 tbsp Wheat Grass	3 tbsp Wheat Grass
Alanine	207 mg	621 mg
Arginine	198 mg	594 mg
Aspartic Acid	150 mg	450 mg
Cysteine	33 mg	99 mg
Glutamine	228 mg	684 mg
Glycine	147 mg	441 mg
Histidine	54 mg	162 mg
Isoleucine	105 mg	315 mg
Leucine	21 mg	63 mg
Lysine	114 mg	342 mg
Methionine	54 mg	162 mg

Phenylalanine	108 mg	324 mg
Proline	138 mg	414 mg
Serine	62 mg	186 mg
Threonine	126 mg	378 mg
Tryptophan	18 mg	54 mg
Tyrosine	99 mg	297 mg
Valine	144 mg	432 mg

These are rough estimates of wheat grass ingredients. Variations in wheat grasses are due to soil conditions. Reports are taken from Wigmore (1985), Schnabel (1935), and independent nutritional analyses of various wheat grass products. Where RDA was not reported, it was not available.

By taking at least 3 tablespoons of wheat grass powder per day throughout the day preferably one tablespoon before each meal, many vital neurological, mental health, and memory support nutrients nearly meet or surpass RDA minimums including: Vitamin A, Vitamin C, zinc, several B vitamins, folic acid, magnesium, phosphorous, glutamine, tyrosine, tryptophan, and selenium. Though I give palatable blender recipe ideas in chapter two for wheat grass, I don't care if you take teaspoons-full dry and wash them down afterwards. I would not suggest that. At least mix the powder with a little water to prevent choking or mix it into other food. The point is get it into yourself or find a viable alternative you can digest with the basics covered from chapter two and this appendix.

The nutrient information in this appendix has not been evaluated by the FDA. Wheat grass and other nutrients here are part of a basic nutrition plan that must be in place first if a thorough memory supplement program is to be of value. These nutrients are not offered as cures of memory loss, but rather as methods of maintaining health that would reduce possibilities of memory loss and other illnesses.

Though there are no claims laid from any one nutrient, there is scientific evidence that corroborates many of these nutritional supports for memory (Null, 1995 & Carper, 2000). Wheat grass has much evidence of positive impact on many diseases and interesting support from Ann Wigmore (1985) regarding its ability to impact those with Alzheimer's. Phosphatidylserine has numerous studies backing its effectiveness in prevention of memory loss especially after many years of use in Europe (Crook & Adderly, 1998; Kidd, 1998; Null, 2000).

The shopping list of supplements to follow are included in rigorous studies of memory involving mental functioning, cells, and nerve transmission. Many of the supplements mentioned are lipids and amino acids normally produced by the body. Some of these decrease as persons age. All of these should be included in caring for memory.

Those taking prescription medications will need supervision from their medical doctor to avoid taking any nutrients that are contraindicated. This information is not intended to replace your professional medical treatment.

To begin this memory supplementation program, turn the page. Take the shopping list to your local health food store or look for these supplements on my website **www.dontforgetmemoryloss.com** or elsewhere over the Internet.

APPENDICES JOYCE

*Memory Support Health Food Store Shopping List

*Phosphatidylserine (PS) (100 mg/ 3 times per day) Must have! Tested, studied, found highly effective!
*Phosphatidylcholine (PC) often mixed in with the **PS**. (500 mg per day) or take **Lecithin**, the purified form.
*Choline (500 mg) Also in lecithin and **PC**. Choose at least one: Choline, lecithin, or PC. Also in wheat grass.
*Vitamin E (800-1000 IU a day) Must have! Important!
*Multi-Vitamin B Complex with folic acid. High potency multiple required. Partially found in wheat grass.
*Omega 3 oils/ Flaxseed (200-650 mg a day) Important!
*Wheat Grass (3-6 tablespoons per day) Has: **Zinc, folic acid, magnesium, phosphorous, glutamine, tyrosine, tryptophan, selenium, etc. (pp. 244-247).**

Develop your personal strategy by adding the following:
Acetyl-L-carnitine (500-1500 mg per day) Effective. Combine with alpha lipoic acid. Promising research.
Alpha lipoic acid (200 mg per day) Powerful, helpful.
COQ10 (100-200 mg per day) Effective cell strengthener.
Vinpocetine (5-10 mg/ 3 times per day) Also excellent! Highly proven. Helpful to memory ailments. All ages.
Huperzine A (Dosages up to 50 mcg four times a day) Higher dose may have side effects; Adolescents also use.
Bacopa Monniera (250 mg/ 3 times per day) Boosts mental clarity, Rejuvenates nerves and brain cells.
Galantamine (8 mg/ 3 times per day) Fights Alzheimer's
Carnosine (± 500 mg) Brain/anti-aging! Helpful even to children, ADHD, epilepsy, or any nerve related problem.
Inositol (500-1000 mg) For anxious, depressed memory.
DHEA (50 mg per day) and **Pregnenolone** (5 mg/day).
Ginseng and **Ginkgo biloba** as directed. Both boost **PS**. These last four also assist menopausal memory.

DON'T FORGET
Bibliography

Amen, D. (1998). *Change your brain change your life.* New York, NY: Three Rivers Press.

American Heart Association. (1994). *Aphasia and the family.* Single copies available free from your local heart association. Publication DM359.

American Psychiatric Association. (1995). *Quick reference to the diagnostic criteria from diagnostic and statistical manual of mental disorders-IV.* Washington, D.C.: American Psychiatric Association.

Anderson, H., & Goolishian, H. (1988). Human systems as linguistic systems: Preliminary and evolving ideas about the implication for clinical theory. *Family Process. 27(4),* 371-393.

Andrews, J., & Andrews, M. (1990). *Family based treatment in communicative disorders: A systemic approach.* Sandwich, IL: Janelle Publications, Inc.

Aronson, J. (1992). *The interface of family therapy and a juvenile arbitration and mediation program.* Unpublished doctoral dissertation, Nova Southeastern University, Fort Lauderdale, Fl.

Asen, K., Berkowitz, R., Cooklin, A., Leff, J., Loader, P., Piper, R., & Rein, L. (1991). Family therapy outcome research: A trial for families, therapists, and researchers. *Family Process, 30,* 3-20.

Aurelia, J. (1980). *Aphasia therapy manual.* Danville, IL: The Interstate Printers & Publishers, Inc.

Bassett, Lucinda. (2000). *Attacking Anxiety and Depression.* Oak Harbor, OH: The Midwest Center.

Bateson, G. (1972). *Steps to an ecology of the mind.* New York, NY: Ballantine Books.

Basso, A., Gardelli, M., Grassi, M., & Mariotti, M. (1989). The role of the right hemisphere in recovery from aphasia: Two case studies. *Cortex, 25*(4), 555-566.

Bauer, R., & Rubens, A. (1985). Agnosia. In K. Heilman & E. Valenstein (Eds.), *Clinical neuropsychology* (pp. 187-242). New York, NY: Oxford.

Bateson, M. C. (1991). Multiple kinds of knowledge: Societal decision-making. In M. J. McGee-Brown (Ed.), *Diversity and design: Studying culture and the individual*
(pp. 1-21). Athens, GA: College of Education, The University of Georgia.

Bateson, M. C. (1994). *With a daughter's eye: A memoir of Margaret Mead and Gregory Bateson.* New York, NY: Harper Collins Publishers.

Bayles, K., & Tomoeda, C. (1990). Delayed recall deficits in aphasic stroke patients: Evidence of Alzheimer's dementia? *Journal of Speech and Hearing Disorders, 55*(2), 310-314.

Benson, D. (1985). Aphasia. In K. Heilman & E. Valenstein (Eds.), *Clinical neuropsychology* (pp.17-41). New York, NY: Oxford.

Birket-Smith, M., Blegvad, N., Knudsen, H., & Nissen, J. (1989). Life events and social support in prediction of stroke outcome. (1989, Madrid, Spain). 10th World Congress of the International College of Psychosomatic Medicine (1989, Madrid, Spain). *Psychotherapy and Psychosomatics, 52*(1-3), 146-150.

Bogdan, R., & Biklen, S. (1982). *Qualitative research for education; Introduction to theory and methods.* Boston, MA: Allyn & Bacon.

Boone, D., Bayles, K., & Koopman, C. (1982).

Communicative aspects of aging. In C. F. Koopman (Ed.), *The otolaryngologic clinics of North America- Vol.15: 2: Symposium on geriatric otolaryngology* (pp. 313-327). Philadelphia, PA: W.B. Saunders.

Boscolo, L., Cecchin, G., Hoffman, L., & Penn, P. (1987) *Milan Systemic Family Therapy: Conversations in Theory and Practice.* New York, NY: Basic Books.

Bowler, J., Hadar, U., & Wade, J. (1994). Cognition in stroke. *Acta Neurologica Scandinavica, 90*(6), 424-429.

Brody, C., & Semel, V. (1993). *Strategies for therapy with the elderly.* New York, NY: Springer Publishing.

Broida, H. (1977). Language therapy effects in long term aphasia. *Archives of Physical Medicine and Rehabilitation, 58,* 248-253.

Brubaker, S. (1982). *Sourcebook for aphasia: A guide to family activities and community resources.* Detroit, MI: Wayne State University Press.

Brubaker, S. (1983). *Workbook for reasoning skills.* Detroit, MI: Wayne State University Press.

Brubaker, S. (1984). *Workbook for language skills.* Detroit, MI: Wayne State University Press.

Brubaker, S. (1985). *Workbook for aphasia: Revised edition.* Detroit, MI: Wayne State University Press.

Brubaker, S. (1987). *Workbook for cognitive skills.* Detroit, MI: Wayne State University Press.

Brumfitt, S. (1993). Losing your sense of self: What aphasia can do. *Aphasiology, 7*(6), 569-575.

Brumfitt, S., Atkinson, J., & Greated, C. (1994). The carer's response to written information about acquired communication problems. *Aphasiology, 8*(6), 583-590.

Carper, J. (2000). *Your miracle brain.* New York, NY: Harper Collins.

Chenail, R. J. (1993). Creating frames and constructing galleries: Charting clinical conversations. In A. H. Rambo, A. Heath, & R. J. Chenail, *Practicing therapy* (pp. 153-224). New York, NY: Norton.

Chenail, R. J. (1994). Qualitative research and clinical work, "Private-ization" and "Public-ation". *The Qualitative Report: An Online Journal Dedicated to Qualitative Research and Critical Inquiry, 2(1).* 1, 3-13. www.nsu.acast.nova.edu/ssss/index.html

Chenail, R. J. (1995). Presenting qualitative data. *The Qualitative Report: An Online Journal Dedicated to Qualitative Research and Critical Inquiry, 2(3),* 1-24. www.nsu.acast.nova.edu/ssss/index.html

Code, C., & Muller, D. (1989). *Aphasia therapy,* (2nd ed). San Diego, CA: Singular Publishing.

Christensen, J., & Anderson, J. (1989). Spouse adjustment to stroke: Aphasic versus nonaphasic partners. *Journal of Communication Disorders, 22*(4), 225-231.

Clare, L. (2002). Relearning face-name associations in early Alzheimer's disease. *Neuropsychology, 16*(4), 538-547.

Constas, M. A. (1992). Qualitative analysis as a public event: The documentation of category development procedures. *American Educational Research Journal, 29*(2), 253-260.

Coll, P. (1989). Depression associated with a stroke. *Journal of Family Practice, 28*(2), 153-155.

Crook, T., & Adderly, B. (1998). *The memory cure.* New York, NY: Pocket Books.

Damasio, H. (1981). Cerebral localization of the aphasia. In M. T. Sarno (Ed.), *Acquired ahasia* (pp. 27-50). New York, NY: Academic Press.

De Vito, J. (1970). *Psychology of speech and language.* New York, NY: Random House.

de Shazer, S. (1991). *Putting difference to work.* New York, NY: Norton.

Donoso, A. (1988). El paciente afasico.The aphasic patient. *Revista Chilena de Neuro Psiquiatria, 26*(1), 46-50.

Draper, B., Poulos, C., Cole, A., & Poulos, R. (1991). A comparison of caregivers for elderly stroke and dementia victims. Annual National Conference of the Australian Association of Gerontology (1991, Sydney, Australia) *Journal of the American Geriatrics Society, 40*(9), 896-901.

Eisenson, J. (1971a). Aphasia in adults: Basic considerations. In L.E. Travis (Ed.), *Handbook of speech pathology and audiology* (pp.1219-1252). Englewood Cliffs, NJ: Prentice-Hall.

Eisenson, J. (1971b). Therapeutic problems and approaches with aphasic adults. In L.E. Travis (Ed.), *Handbook of speech pathology and audiology* (pp.1253-1276). Englewood Cliffs, NJ: Prentice-Hall.

Eisenson, J. (1984). *Adult aphasia: Assessment and treatment.* New York, NY: Appleton Century Crofts.

Evans, R., Matlock, A., Bishop, D., Stranahan, S., & Pederson, C. (1988). Family intervention after stroke: Does counseling or education help? *Stroke, 19,* 1243-1249.

Evans, R., Connis, R., Bishop, D., & Hendricks, R. (1994). Stroke: A family dilemma. Special Issue:

Disability and rehabilitation in older persons. *Disability and Rehabilitation An International Multidisciplinary Journal, 16*(3), 110-118.

Fiebel, J., & Springer, C. (1982). Depression and failure to resume social activities after stroke. *Archives of Physical Medicine and Rehabilitation, 63*, 276-278.

Fisch, R., Weakland, J. & Segal, L. (1982). San Francisco, CA: Jossey-Bass Publishers.

Foster, N. (1987). Age-related changes in the human nervous system. In H.G. Mueller and V.C. Geoffrey (Eds.), *Communication disorders in aging* (pp.3-35). Washington, DC: Gallaudet University Press.

Frankl, V. (1992). *Man's search for significance.* Boston, MA: Beacon Press.

Gale, J., & Newfield, N. (1992). A conversation analysis of a solution focused marital therapy session. *Journal of Marital and Family Therapy, 18*, 153-165.

Gardner, H. (1975). *The shattered mind: The person after brain damage.* New York, NY: Alfred A. Knopf.

Geddes, J., Chamberlain, M., & Bonsall, M. (1991). The Leeds Family Placement Scheme: Principles, participants and postscript. *Clinical Rehabilitation, 5*(1), 53-64.

Geddes, J., & Chamberlain, M. (1989). The Leeds Family Placement Scheme: An evaluation of its use as a rehabilitation resource. *Clinical Rehabilitation, 3*(3), 189-197.

Glaser, B., & Strauss, A. (1967). *The discovery of grounded theory: Strategies for qualitative research.* New York, NY: Aldine.

Grober, E., & Buschke, H. (1987). Genuine

memory deficits in dementia. *Developmental Neuropsychology, 3*, 13-36.

Guba, E. (1978). *Toward a methodology of naturalistic inquiry in educational evaluation.* CSE Monograph Series in Evaluation No. 8. Los Angeles: University of California, Los Angeles, CA: Center for the Study of Evaluation.

Haggstrom,T., Axelsson, K., & Norberg, A. (1994). The experience of living with stroke sequelae illuminated by means of stories and metaphors. *Qualitative Health Research, 4*(3), 321-337.

Hansen, V. (1957). Social and emotional aspects of aphasia. *Journal of Speech and Hearing Disorders, 22,* 53-59.

Hartbauer, R. (1978). *Counseling in communicative disorders.* Springfield, IL: Charles C. Thomas.

Heilman, K., & Valenstein, E. (1985). *Clinical Neuropsychology.* New York, NY: Oxford.

Herrmann, M., Bartels, C., & Wallesch, C. (1993). Depression in acute and chronic aphasia: Symptoms, pathoanatomical-clinical correlations and functional implications. *Journal of Neurology, Neurosurgery and Psychiatry, 56*(6), 672-678.

Herrman, M., Britz, A, Bartels, C., & Wallesch, C. (1995). The impact of aphasia on the patient and family in the first year post stroke. *Topics in Stroke Rehabilitation, 2*(3), 5-19.

Herz, F. (1989). The impact of death and serious illness on the family life cycle. In E.A. Carter & M. McGoldrick (Eds.), *The family life cycle: A framework for family therapy* (2nd ed.). Boston, MA: Allyn and Bacon.

Hinckley, J. (1995). Alternative family education programming for adults with chronic aphasia. *Topics in Stroke Rehabilitation, 2*(3), 33-52.

Holland, A., & Beeson, P. (1993). Finding a new sense of self: What the clinician can do to help. *Aphasiology, 7*(6), 581-584.

Hopper, R. (1988). Speech, for instance. The exemplar in studies in conversation. *Journal of Language and Social Psychology, 4*(1), 36-63.

Hough, M. (1993). Treatment of Wernicke's Aphasia with jargon: A case study. *Journal of Communication Disorders, 26*, 101-111.

Hunsley, J. (1993). Research and family therapy: Exploring some hidden assumptions. *Journal of Systemic Therapies, 12*(1), 63-70.

Iskowitz, M. (1998a). Reduced opportunities for communication following aphasia can lead to feelings of depression. *Advance for Speech-Language Pathologists & Audiologists, 8*(24), 12-14.

Iskowitz, M. (1998b). Restoring speech and swallow control:Assessment criteria for speaking valve use among patients with trach and ventilator dependency. *Advance for Speech-Language Pathologists & Audiologists, 8*(30), 6-7.

Jenkins, C. D. (1992). Assessment of outcomes of health intervention. *Social Science Medicine, 35*(4), 367-375.

Jongbloed, L. (1994). Adaptation to a stroke: The experience of one couple. *American Journal of Occupational Therapy, 48*(11), 1006-1013.

DON'T FORGET

Keith, R. (1984a). *Speech and language rehabilitation: A workbook for the neurologically impaired,* Volume I. Danville, IL: The Interstate Printers and Publishers, Inc.

Keith, R. (1984b). *Speech and language rehabilitation: A workbook for the neurologically impaired,* Volume 2. Danville, IL: The Interstate Printers and Publishers, Inc.

Kertesz, A., & McCabe, P. (1977). Recovery patterns and prognosis in aphasia. *Brain, 100,* 1-18.

Kertesz, A. (1985). Recovery and treatment. In K. Heilman & E. Valenstein (Eds.), *Clinical Neuropsychology.* New York, NY: Oxford.

Kettle, M., & Chamberlain, M. (1989). The stroke patient in an urban environment. *Clinical Rehabilitation. 3*(2), 131-138.

Kidd, P. M. (1998). *Phosphatidylserine: The nutrient building block that accelerates all brain functions and counters Alzheimer's.* New Canaan, CT: Keats Publishing.

Kilpatrick, K. (1979). *Therapy guide for the adult with language and speech disorders: Volume II, advanced stimulus materials.* Akron, OH: Visiting Nurse Service.

Kilpatrick, K., & Jones, C. (1977). *Therapy guide for the adult with language and speech disorders: Volume I, a selection of stimulus materials.* Akron, OH: Visiting Nurse Service.

Kinney, J., Stephens, M., Franks, M., & Norris, V. (1995). Stresses and satisfactions of family caregivers to older stroke patients. *Journal of Applied Gerontology, 14*(1), 3-21.

Kleinman, A. (1988). *The illness narrative:*

Suffering, healing, and the human condition. New York, NY: Basic Books.

Knox, D. (1985). *Portrait of aphasia.* Detroit, MI: Wayne State University Press.

Koivisto, K., Viinamaki, H., & Riekkinen, P. (1993). Poststroke depression and rehabilitation outcome. *Nordic Journal of Psychiatry, 47*(4), 245-249.

Kosslyn, S., & Koenig, O. (1992). *Wet mind: The new cognitive neuroscience.* New York, NY: The Free Press.

Kubler-Ross, E. (1969). *On Death and Dying.* New York, NY: Macmillan.

Kuzel, A. J. (1992). Sampling in qualitative inquiry. In B. F. Crabtree & W. L. Miller (Eds.), *Doing qualitative research.* Newbury Park, CA: Sage.

Labi, M., Phillips, T., & Gresham, G. (1980). Psychosocial disability in physically restored long term stroke survivors. *Archives of Physical Medicine and Rehabilitation, 61,* 561-565.

Lang, C., Berendes, T., Sauerbrei, W., & Bartelsen, P. (1989). Is aphasia a significant prognostic factor for the recovery of function after ischemic stroke causing hemiparesis? *Journal of Neurologic Rehabilitation, 3*(4),177-186.

LeDorze, G., Julien, M., Brassard, C., & Durocher, J. (1994). An analysis of the communication of adult residents of a long-term care hospital as perceived by their caregivers. *European Journal of Disorders of Communication, 29*(3), 241-268.

Leininger, M. (1985). Ethnography and ethnonursing models and modes of qualitative data analysis. In M. Leininger (Ed.), *Qualitative research methods in nursing* (pp. 50-71). Orlando, FL: Grune & Stratton, Inc.

Lichtenberg, P., & Rosenthal, M. (1994). Characteristics of geriatric rehabilitation programs: A survey of practitioners. *Rehabilitation Psychology, 39*(4), 277-281.

Lincoln, N., Jones, A., & Mulley, G. (1985). Psychological effects of speech therapy. *Journal of Psychosomatic Research, 29,* 467-474.

Lincoln, Y. S. (1995). Emerging criteria for quality in qualitative and interpretive research. *Qualitative Inquiry, 1*(3), 275-289.

Lincoln, Y. S., & Guba, E. G. (1985). *Naturalistic inquiry.* Beverly Hills, CA: Sage.

Mackenzie, C. (1993). Concern for the aphasic person's sense of self: Why, who and how? *Aphasiology, 7*(6), 584-589.

Mahrer, A.R. (1988). Discovery-oriented psychotherapy research: Rationale, aims, and methods. *American Psychologist, 43*(9), 694-702.

Mapelli, G., Pavoni, M., & Ramelli, E. (1980). Emotional and psychotic reactions induced by aphasia. *Psychiatria Clinica, 13,* 108-118.

Mark, V., & Mark, J. (1989). *Brain power: A neurosurgeon's complete program to maintain and enhance brain fitness throughout your life.* Boston: Houghton Mifflin.

Marks, M., Taylor, M., & Rusk, L. (1957). Rehabilitation of the aphasic patient's survey of three years' experience in a rehabilitation setting. *Neurology, 7,* 837-843.

Maxwell, J. A. (1992). Understanding and validity

in qualitative research. *Harvard Educational Review, 62,* 279-300.

McClenahan, R., Johnston, M., & Densham, Y. (1990). Misperceptions of comprehension difficulties of stroke patients by doctors, nurses and relatives. *Journal of Neurology, Neurosurgery and Psychiatry, 53*(8), 700-701.

McClenahan, R., Johnston, M., & Densham, Y. (1992). Factors influencing accuracy of estimation of comprehension problems in patients following cerebrovascular accident, by doctors, nurses and relatives. *European Journal of Disorders of Communication, 27*(3), 209-219.

McDaniel, S., Hepworth, J., & Doherty, W. (1992). *Medical family therapy: A biopsychosocial approach to families with health problems.* New York, NY: Basic Books.

McGoldrick, M., & Gerson, R. (1985). *Genograms in Family Assessment.* New York, NY: Norton Press.

McKhann, G., & Albert, M. (2002). *Keep your brain young.* New York, NY: Wiley

Merriam, S. B. (1990). Dealing with validity, reliability, and ethics in case study research. In *Case study research in education* (pp. 163-184). San Francisco, CA: Jossey-Bass.

Mesulam, M.M. (1982). Slowly progressive aphasia without generalized dementia. *Annals of Neurology, 11,* 592-598.

Miceli, G., Caltagirone, C., Gainotti, G., Masullo, C., Silveri, M.C., & Villa, G. (1981). Influence of age, sex, literacy, and pathologic lesion on incidence, severity and type of aphasia. *Acta Neurologica Scandinavica,* 64,

370-382.

Miller, L. (1991). The "other" brain injuries: Psychotherapeutic issues with stroke and brain tumor patients. *Cognitive Rehabilitation, 9*(5), 10-16.

Miller, W., & Crabtree, B. (1992). Primary care research: A multimethod typology and qualitative road map. In B. Crabtree & W. Miller (Eds.), *Doing qualitative research* (pp. 233-255). Newbury Park, CA: Sage.

Mishler, E. G. (1986a). Language, meaning, and narrative analysis. In *Research interviewing: Context and narrative* (pp. 66-116). Cambridge, MA: Harvard University Press.

Mishler, E. G. (1986b). Research interviews as speech events: The joint construction of meaning. In *Research interviewing: Context and narrative* (pp. 35-65). San Francisco, CA: Jossey-Bass.

Mishler, E. G. (1986c). The analysis of interview-narratives. In T. Sarbin (Ed.). *Narrative psychology*. New York, NY: Praeger.

Montgomery-West, P. (1995). A spouse's perspective on life with aphasia. *Topics in Stroke Rehabilitation, 2*(3), 1-4.

Morris, P., Robinson, R., Raphael, B., & Bishop, D. (1991). The relationship between the perception of social support and post-stroke depression in hospitalized patients. *Psychiatry, 54*(3), 306-316.

Morris, P., Robinson, R., Raphael, B., & Samuels, J. (1992). The relationship between risk factors for affective disorder and poststroke depression in hospitalized stroke patients. *Australian and New Zealand Journal of Psychiatry, 26*(2), 208-217.

Mueller, H., & Geoffrey, V. (1987).

Communication disorders in aging Washington, DC: Gallaudet University Press.

Mulhall, D. (1988). The management of the aphasic patient. In F.C. Rose, R. Whurr & M.A. Wyke (Eds.), *Aphasia* (pp.459-517). London: Whurr.

Mysak, E., & Hanley, T. (1958). Aging process in speech: Pitch and duration characteristics. *Journal of Gerontology, 13*, 309-313.

National Aphasia Association. (1988). *Impact of aphasia on patients and family: Results of a needs survey.* New York, NY.

Naeser, M., Gaddie, A., Palumbo, C., & Stiassny-Eder, D. (1990). Late recovery of auditory comprehension in global aphasia: Improved recovery observed with subcortical temporal isthmus lesion vs Wernicke's cortical area lesion. American Speech, Language, and Hearing Association Meetings (1987, New Orleans, Louisiana). *Archives of Neurology, 47*(4), 425-432.

Nelson, T., Fleuridas, C., & Rosenthal, D. (1986). The evolution of circular questions: Training family therapists. *Journal of Marital and Family Therapy, 12*(2), 113-127.

Norris, V., Stephens, M., & Kinney, J. (1986). The impact of family interactions on recovery from stroke: Help or hindrance? *Gerontologist, 30*(4), 535-542.

Null, G. (2000). *Food-mood body connection.* New York, NY: Seven Stories Press.

Opie, A. (1991). The informal caregivers of the confused elderly and the concept of partnership: A New Zealand report. *Pride Institute Journal of Long Term Home Health Care, 10*(2), 34-40.

Osgoode, C., & Miron, M. (1963). *Approaches to the study of aphasia.* Chicago, IL: University of Illinois Press.

Overman, C., & Geoffrey, V. (1987). Alzheimer's disease and other dementias. In H.G. Mueller and V.C. Geoffrey (Eds.), *Communication disorders in aging* (pp. 271-297). Washington, DC: Gallaudet University Press.

Parr, S. (1994). Coping with aphasia: Conversations with 20 aphasic people. *Aphasiology, 8*(5), 457-466.

Patton, M. Q. (1990). *Qualitative research evaluation methods* (2nd ed.). Newbury Park, CA: Sage.

Peach, R. (1987). Language functioning. In H.G. Mueller & V.C. Geoffrey (Eds.), *Communication disorders in aging* (pp. 238-270). Washington, DC: Gallaudet University Press.

Pepper, C. (1987). Foreword. In H.G. Mueller & V.C. Geoffrey (Eds.), *Communication disorders in aging* (pp.vii-viii). Washington, DC: Gallaudet University Press.

Periard, M., & Ames, B. (1993). Lifestyle changes and coping patterns among caregivers of stroke survivors. *Public Health Nursing, 10*(4), 252-256.

Peterson, C. (1981). *Conversation starters.* Danville, IL: The Interstate Printers & Publishers.

Polkinghorne, D. (1988). *Narrative knowing and the human sciences.* Albany, NY: State University of New York, NY Press.

Pound, P., Gompertz, P., & Ebrahim, S. (1993). Development and results of a questionnaire to measure career satisfaction after stroke. *Journal of Epidemiology and Community Health, 47*(6), 500-505.

Reisman, C. (1993). *Narrative Analysis.*

Qualitative research methods series, No. 30. Newbury Park, CA: Sage.

Reitan, R., & Wolfson, D. (1992). *Neuroanatomy and Neuropathology: A Clinical Guide for Neuropsychologists.* Tucsan, AR: Neuropsychology Press.

Rice, B., Paul, A., & Muller, D. (1987). An evaluation of a social support group for spouses of aphasic partners. *Aphasiology, 1,* 247-256.

Robbins, A. (2000). *Get the edge.* San Diego, CA: Robbins Research International, Inc.

Robinson, R., & Price, T. (1982). Post-stroke depressive disorders: Follow-up study of 103 patients. *Stroke, 13,* 635-641.

Robinson, R., Bolduc, P., Kubos, K., Starr, L., & Price, T. (1985). Social functioning assessment in stroke patients. *Archives of Physical Medicine and Rehabilitation, 66,* 496-500.

Roeltgen, D. (1985). Agraphia. In K.Heilman & E.Valenstein (Eds.), *Clinical Neuropsychology* (pp. 75-84). New York, NY: Oxford.

Rolland, J. (1992). *Families, illness, and disability: An integrative treatment model.* New York, NY: Basic Books.

Rossi, E. (2002). *The Psychobiology of gene expression: Neuroscience and neurogenesis in hypnosis and the healing arts.* New York, NY: W.W. Norton & Co.

Sarno, J., & Sarno, M. (1979). *Stroke: A guide for patients and their families.* (rev. ed.) New York, NY: McGraw-Hill.

Sarno, M. (1993). Aphasia rehabilitation: Psychosocial and ethical considerations. *Aphasiology, 7*(4), 321-334.

Sarno, M., & Levita, E. (1971). Natural course of recovery in severe aphasia. *Archives of Physical Medicine and Rehabilitation, 52*, 175-179.

Schnabel, C. (1935). *The biologic value of high protein cereal grasses.* Paper presented to the biologic section of the American Chemical Society in New York, April 22, 1935.

Schuell, H. (1974). An introduction to the study of aphasia. In L. Sies (Ed.), *Aphasia theory and therapy: Selected lectures and papers of Hildred Schuell* (pp. 1-67). Baltimore, MD: University Park Press.

Schuell, H. (1974). Clinical symptoms of aphasia. In L. Sies (Ed.), *Aphasia theory and therapy: Selected lectures and papers of Hildred Schuell* (pp. 157-172). Baltimore, MD: University Park Press.

Schuell, A., Jenkins, J., & Jimenez-Pabon, J. (1964). *Aphasia in adults.* New York, NY: Harper & Row.

Selkoe, D. (2002). Alzheimer's disease is a synaptic failure. *Science, 298,* 789-791.

Sharpe, M., Hawton, K., Seagroatt, V., & Bamford, J. (1994). Depressive disorders in long-term survivors of stroke: Associations with demographic and social factors, functional status, and brain lesion volume. Special Issue: Depression. *British Journal of Psychiatry, 164,* 380-386.

Shimberg, E. (1990). *Strokes: What families should know.* New York, NY: Ballantine Books.

Small, G. (2002). *The memory bible.* New York, NY: Hyperion.

Smith, A., Chamoux, R., Leri, J., London, R., & Muraski, A. (1972). *Diagnosis, intelligence and rehabilitation of chronic aphasics.* Ann Arbor, MI: University of Michigan Department of Physical Medicine and Rehabilitation.

Snowdon, D., Kemper, S., Mortimer, J., Greiner, L., Wekstein, D. & Markesbery, W. Linguistic ability in early life and cognitive function and Alzheimer's disease in later life. Findings from the nun study. *Journal of the American Medical Association,* 275, (7) 528-532.

Spreen, O., Risser, A., & Edgell, D. (1995). *Developmental neuropsychology.* New York, NY: Oxford.

Stiell, K., & Gillian, G. (1995). Co-therapy with couples affected by aphasia. *Topics in Stroke Rehabilitation, 2*(3), 34-38.

Strauss, A., & Corbin, J. (1994). Grounded theory methodology. In N. K. Denzin & Y. S. Lincoln (Eds.), *Handbook of qualitative research* (pp. 273-285). London: Sage.

Stryker, S. (1981). *Speech after stroke: A manual for the speech pathologist and the family member.* Springfield, IL: Charles C. Thomas.

Tagg, S. K. (1985). Lifestory interviews and their interpretations. In M. Brenner, J. Brown, & D. Canter (Eds.), *The research interview: Uses and approaches.* London: Academic Press.

Tanner, D. (1980). Loss and grief: implications for the speech-language pathologist and audiologist. *Journal of the American Speech and Hearing Association, 22,* 916-928.

Taylor, M. (1958). *Understanding aphasia: A guide for family and friends* (pamphlet). New York, NY: Institute of rehabilitation medicine, NY University

Medical Center, 400 E. 34 St., New York, NY.

Taylor, S., & Bogdan, R. (1984). *Introduction to qualitative research methods: The search for meaning* (2nd ed.). New York, NY: Wiley.

Tomlinson, B., Blessed, G., & Roth, M. (1970). Observations on the brains of demented old people. *Journal of the Neurological Sciences, 11,* 205-242.

Traustadottir, R. (1991). Mothers who care: Gender, disability, and family life. *Journal of Family Issues, 12*(2), 211-228.

Uffen, E. (1998). Closeup. *Asha: The Magazine of the American Speech Language Hearing Association,* Winter, 14.

Wahrborg, P. (1991). *Assessment and management of emotional and psychosocial reactions to brain damage and aphasia.* Kilworth: Fax Communications.

Watzlawick, P., Weakland, J., & Fisch, R. (1974). *Change: Principles of Problem Formation and Problem Resolution.* New York, NY: W.W. Norton & Co.

Weiss, M. (1994). *The continuing story: Life with a child with autism.* A dissertation presented to Nova Southeastern University. Fort Lauderdale, FL: Nova Southeastern University.

White, M., & Epston, D. (1990). *Narrative means to therapeutic ends.* New York, NY: W.W. Norton & Co.

Wigmore, A. (1985). *The wheatgrass book.* Wayne, NJ: Avery.

Yanko, J. (1987). Neurologic disorders. In nursing 87 books series, *Patient teaching* (pp. 1-4). Springhouse, PA: Springhouse Corporation.

INDEX

A
AAMI...12-33, 24, 244-248
anti-aging...12-33
acetylcholine...13, 34
acute aphasia...113-114
ADHD...27
aluminum...14
Alzheimer's...4-6
Alzheimer's
   acetylcholine...13, 34
   hippocampus... 13, 34
   therapy after ...4-5
   genetics of ...26
amnesias... 6, 33-34, 221, 226, see also head injury
anger...123, 207-208
anxiety...18
aphasia...2, 32, 33, 36-41, 221, 229-249, Ch. 5, 6, App. A, B, C, & D
appropriate materials...214
apraxia...224, 226
articulation...46
audio-books 92
   reading out loud..46, 126, 213

B
behaviors of children 136-152
benzodiazepines...17
body language...215-216
brain damage...195, 200-201
brain tumors...27

C
career related 161-171
children
` discipline... 76, 136-152
  helpers... 48, 136-152
cigarettes...16
coffee...16
computers..46, 54, 126, 212, 216
   Email...55
   handheld PDA46, 216
   Internet resource...54-55, 212, 232-234
   software..212
   lingraphica...46, 216
comprehension.63-65, 113-115
concerns...82-194
coping...
   at start...98
   psychological.171-193
   criticism...
coumadin...24, 132, 173-174, 189
cures...25

D
death...63-65, 74, 156, 162-164
definitions of terms 222-226
   acalculia...225
   agnosia...222
   agrammatism. .
   agraphia...225
   alexia....224
   anomia...223
   aphasia...221
   apraxia...223, 226
   astereognosis...225
   comprehension...65
   dementia...226
   dysgnosia...222
   dysgraphia...225
   dysphagia,,169-170, 226
   dyslexia...224
   dysnomia...223

dysstereogosis...226
expressive aphasia.222
jargon...226, 228
neologisms...226, 228
paraphasias...226, 228
perseveration...161-162, 226, 228
receptive aphasia...221
dementia ...222
    inappropriate label ...5
demographics...60
depression...188, 208
diagnosis...117, 210
    classifications...3-6, 27-32, 221-230
driving...164
drug abuse...27, 17, 18
drug companies. 19-28
drugs and vitamins...15, 17, 19-20, 24, 12-32
dysphagia..116, 169-170, 226

E
Education....73, 82-99
E-mail...55
emotions...207-208
epilepsy...31, 233-234
    nutrients...31, 244-248
expectations...82-99, 210
    importance of...57-59, 210

F
family concerns
    See Ch. 6
    Tina's head injury..195
    Danny's accident ...200
    Kaye - helpful metaphor 161, 171, 186
    Laura's support

    saved Steve...129, 158, 207
family project 48,141,120-121, 202
    beginnings73, 203,216
    endings...203
    pick appropriate materials...212-214
    mental exercise...201
    teamwork...48, 121, 149 206
family solutions...231-249
    body language...215
    eye contact...49
    first sound prompt..52
    plateaus happen...50
    think before talking..51, 64
    no pressure in public.51
family support systems, movies regarding
    with...205
    without...205
family therapy...157, 160, 183, 215
fears...130-135
financial hardship.161-170, 200-203, 212-213
forgetting...200
friends...168

G
genetics...26
grieving...74, 208

H
handheld PDA..46
head injury 1-7, 33-39, 41-64, 195-214,

head injury (con't) 229-249, Ch. 7, App. A, C, & D.
healing...214
HIV...27
hope... 57-59, 74, 120, 208-210
hospitals...8, 64, 82-83
  early attention...83
  informing ..82
hospital memory loss protocol...8, 90, 92
hospital...41, 181
  stay discoveries..42, 61
  last words if death...63-65
  ventilator...63-65
hippocampus...34
humor...56

I
informing of memory loss...7, 82-83, 93
insurance...3-10, 35, 70- 74, 90-92, 124-129, 178-179, 184, 190, 194, 210-212
insurance...90, 92, 205
  managed care...2-10,70
  Medicare...47
  negative therapy reports 210
  interfere with benefits 210
  new dilemma for...35
  irresponsible...74, 125, 129, 205
Internet resource...54-55, 232-234

J
jargon...50, 78, 207, 226, 228

K
Keller, Helen...184
Korsakoff's syndrome..15, 26

L
lingraphica laptop...46
living arrangements 136-144
long-term memory 16-17, 26
long-term cases...72-74
  decisions..143, 150, 158
losses (see all chapter 6)

M
marijuana...18
marriage...146-150, 160
medical issues...129
medical doctors 17-18, 27, 29, 31, 32, 27, 64, 70-72, 89-93, 124-125-129, 158-159, 178-179, 194- 199, 205-211
  order therapy...89, 129, 158, 207
  neurologist..173, 196-197
  psychiatrists...17-18, 161, 181-184, 193-194
  surgeon...158-159
Medicare...47
Memento...205
mental exercises...6, 235- 243, 231-234
memory loss
  causes...2-6, 12-32
  distinctions...2
  diagnosis...3, 5-6
  glossary...221-226
memory loss, overlooked 12-18
  AAMI, aging...12-26
  ADHD...27
  brain tumors...27

epilepsy...31
thyroid disorder...29
hormone imbalance...32
depression 18
anger...18
anxiety...18
memory shopping list.248
memory-training...45-58, 89-93, 97, 118, 127-129, 158, 183-184, 194-195, 201, 210-215, 235 see speech therapy
   audio-books, reading out loud..213
   prompting, cuing...51-52
   refresher course...53
   Internet ..231-234
mental distress...171-200
   depression...208
   grieving...208
   to speak or not to speak 209
   value of communication 100-108
mercury...14
metaphors 41, 108, 153-155, 173, 185
   academic challenge.209
   foreign language...41-58
   money...215-216
motivate...119, 128, 159, 201

N
negative therapy reports...210
negativity...54, 200, 207
neologisms...226, 228
neurologist...197-198

nutrition, memory
   vitamins...24-25
   RDA comparison chart...244
   vitamins/minerals...248
nutrition
   wheat grass...244-248
nursing home. 143, 150, 158, 205

O
overlooked memory losses 26-32
overlapping losses...67, 170

P
paraphasia...226, 228
parenting...149
   step-parenting... 138, 147
patience ...56
perseveration...226
personality...161-170
phosphatidylserine/PS..13, 22, 248
phosphatidylcholine/PC.13, 22, 248
plateau, learning...91, 195
prayer...244, 186, 171
prevention..12-32, 244-248
professional & psychological healthcare.171-194, 205
prognosis, ignore..125,129, 159, 208-210
prompting...52
prozac...17
psychological, solutions for 171-193
   anger...207-208
   be here now...199
   body language...215

INDEX

psychological (con't)
  break down...19
  can't believe...195-210,
  criticism/attitude...204
  denial...187
  depression...188,199, 208
  emotions...199, 208
  grieving...208
  hopefulness...194, 208
  negativity...207
  therapy..179-184, 191-198
public speaking...25,
  103, 210, 234
R
recipe ideas...23
referrals...211
recovery time...113, 211
Reeve, Christopher...70,
  201
Regarding Henry...205
rehabilitation...90, 118-
  129, 178-179
  time-line...211
relationship losses...153-
  159, 161-170
role reversals..146-152
S
self directed...91-92, 114,
  122, 189
self-fulfilling prophecy.. 93
sexuality...155-156
short-term memory 17, 26,
  62
smoking...16
social...168
speech therapy...45-58, 89-
  93, 97, 118, 127-129, 158,
  183-184, 194-195, 201, 210-
  215, 235, see memory-
  training and App. C & D.

JOYCE

spiritual ...75, 102, 105-
  106, 128, 155, 171-173, 185-
  188, 218, 244
suicide...181-182, 193-194
support...74, 171-193
stem cell research...70, 201
stress...18, 99, 199
stroke club...180
stuttering...209, 226
support groups...55, 174-177,
  180, 183, 193, 214-
  215, 232
synapses...26, 32, 214
T
therapy..179-184, 191-198
times per day... 21-23, 53, 211
tips...45-58, 213-214, 235
  audio-books..92, 213
  prompting...52
  read/talk aloud...39, 213
  sing...92, 213
  phone codes...123
  yes-no cards...123
Toastmaster's...25, 103, 210
  234
toxins...13-19
thyroid disorders...29-30
V
ventilators...62-65
valves, speech...62-65
vision...214
vitamins...23, 244, 248
W
wheat grass...244, 248
workbooks...212, 231-234
writing...169-170
  journaling...54

1-800-957-0559

Contact the Author

Dr. Jill Joyce has the unusual distinction of being dual licensed in both Psychotherapy and Speech/Language Pathology. Also as a college professor teaching on the topics of memory loss, anti-aging, and neurology, she has research, clinical experience, and personal knowledge of memory loss. She has helped her own mother with age-associated memory impairment and lived alone with her aging grandmother when she had Alzheimer's. Her past clinical work involving persons with memory loss includes: aphasia, stroke, head injury, thyroid disorders, age-associated memory impairment (AAMI), learning disabilities, ADHD, bi-polar, anxiety disorders, depression, Alzheimer's, epilepsy, and substance and hormone related memory losses. Therefore, she is uniquely positioned as one who has viewed and studied the memory loss problem from many different vantage points. She is available to speak to your group on the subject of memory loss and its many unusual forms, offering causes, therapeutic treatments, prevention, and management strategies. In addition, she is also available to you by appointment for therapy and coaching at her virtual office with mytherapynet.com, the referral site of the Dr. Phil show. The link is directly provided from Dr. Joyce's web site www.dontforgetmemoryloss.com. There she also coaches in life and learning management, spirituality, weight loss, memory-training strategies, and relationship issues.

Don't Forget Memory Loss Solutions, Inc.
P.O. Box 670686, Coral Springs, FL 33067
Voice Messaging: **1-800-957-0559**

Website: www.dontforgetmemoryloss.com
E-Mail: dontforget@bellsouth.net

1-800-957-0559

Quick Order Form

Phone: (Have credit card ready)
Internet: www.dontforgetmemoryloss.com
dontforget@bellsouth.net
Mail: Send this form with check or your credit card information to:
Don't Forget Memory Loss Solutions, Inc.
P. O. Box 670686
Coral Springs, FL 33067

Please send _____ copies of the Still Waters Publication:

Don't Forget by Dr. Jill Joyce, Ph.D.

Company _____
Name _____
Address _____
City _____ **State** _____ **Zip** _____
Phone _____ - _____ - _____
E-Mail _____

FL Sales Tax Add 6% books if shipped within Florida
Price: $19.95. Add $1.20   plus shipping
Shipping US: Add $4 for 1st book and $2 for each added
International: Add $9 for the 1st book and $5 for each added

Total $ _____ Enclose check to: Don't Forget MLS, Inc.

To order by credit card *(Please check one)*
   Visa   American Express   Master Card
Name on card _____
Account Number _____
Expiration Date _____
Signature _____

1-800-957-0559

Quick Order Form

Phone:	(Have credit card ready)
Internet:	www.dontforgetmemoryloss.com
	dontforget@bellsouth.net
Mail:	Send this form with check or your credit card information to:
	Don't Forget Memory Loss Solutions, Inc.
	P. O. Box 670686
	Coral Springs, FL 33067

Please send _____ copies of the Still Waters Publication:

Don't Forget by Dr. Jill Joyce, Ph.D.

Company_____
Name_____
Address_____
City_____State_____Zip_____
Phone _____-_____-_____
E-Mail _____

FL Sales Tax Add 6% books if shipped within Florida
Price: $19.95. Add $1.20   plus shipping
Shipping US: Add $4 for 1st book and $2 for each added
International: Add $9 for the 1st book and $5 for each added

Total $ _____   Enclose check to: Don't Forget MLS, Inc.

To order by credit card *(Please check one)*

   Visa   American Express   Master Card
Name on card_____
Account Number_____
Expiration Date_____
Signature _____\